RUSSELL
*Maverick
with a Heart*
Crowe

Stone Wallace
& Nicholle Carrière

ICON
PRESS

© 2005 by Icon Press
First printed in 2005 10 9 8 7 6 5 4 3 2 1
Printed in Canada

The Publisher: Icon Press, an imprint of Folklore Publishing

Website: www.folklorepublishing.com

Library and Archives Canada Cataloguing in Publication

Wallace, Stone, 1957–
   Russell Crowe: maverick with a heart / Stone Wallace and Nicholle Carrière.

(Star biographies)
Includes bibliographical references.
ISBN 1-894864-19-0

   1. Crowe, Russell, 1964– 2. Actors—Australia—Biography.
I. Carrière, Nicholle, 1961– II. Title.

PN3018.C76W34 2005   791.4302'8'092   C2005-900614-5

Project Director: Faye Boer
Production: Trina Koscielnuk, Linda Bolger
Project Editor: Nicholle Carrière, Faye Boer
Cover Design: Valentino
Book Design: Anne & Dion

Cover Image: International Communications Systems

Photography credits: Every effort has been made to accurately credit the sources of photographs. Any errors or omissions should be directed to the publisher for changes in future editions. Photographs courtesy of International Communications Systems.

We acknowledge the support of the Alberta Foundation for the Arts for our publishing program.

PC:P6

Table of Contents

Dedication

Dedicated with love to my stepson, Curtis C. Urbanowich, who urged me to get on with the project

Defining Russell Crowe

At just over 40 years of age, Russell Crowe has become one of the most popular, respected and highest-paid actors in the motion picture industry. His movies invariably receive strong critical notice, while his performances have been positively appraised and applauded around the globe. He can truly be regarded as an international superstar.

But the question remains: Who is Russell Crowe?

He is an actor difficult to define because he refuses to be pigeonholed. To date, his screen work spans a mere 15 years, but Russell has amassed credits that are envied by others of his generation—perhaps not the quantity of his work, but certainly the quality.

Before examining the complexity of his film performances, it's necessary to first take a look at the complexities of the man.

Up until just recently, Russell Crowe had achieved notoriety as one of Hollywood's "bad boys," publicized as a latter-day independent offshoot from the notorious "Brat Pack" of the 1980s, whose onscreen talents paled alongside their oft-hyped offscreen antics. Russell Crowe's ascent into movie superstardom occurred some years later, when Emilio Estevez, his brother Charlie Sheen and Canadian-born Kiefer Sutherland had more or less tempered their carousing. If Russell had emerged during their heyday, he would surely have received immediate membership to their club. Russell was regarded as a pugnacious presence, certainly possessed of a rebellious temperament, a rock-and-roller whose aggressive behavior was often attributed to his "angry young man" persona, perhaps his way of coming to grips with the spotlight suddenly being thrust upon him.

Fortunately, there was a counterbalance—the sheer joy and challenge he received from acting. Russell Crowe avows that he is dedicated to his craft, not his celebrity status, although when one reaches superstar status, it is difficult to have a clear dividing line. Russell works both to satisfy an artistic need and to entertain his audience. He has battled his own inner demons and therefore is not afraid to present the layers of psychology and emotion that exist in all of us as humans, along with the social conditions that shape and change us. Each of us identifies with the human truths inherent in many of Russell Crowe's screen characterizations, but we must also appreciate the heavy burden that his craft imposes on him. Each role—regardless of whether it depicts positive or negative qualities— is absorbed into his psyche and hopefully receives outlet through the creative experience. However, it leaves a lasting impression on the actor, establishing references that can be called upon in later characterizations.

> Life experiences shape each of us into individuals. Actors learn to appreciate, recognize and expand upon each day's trials and triumphs. An actor's greatest responsibility is to bring us "beyond ourselves," to allow us to experience, respect or despise the distinguishing moments of another's life.

Hence, the keyword to Russell Crowe's success is versatility. There are few actors today who can match, let alone surpass, the dramatic range of Russell Crowe. Russell provides his audiences not merely with entertainment, but also film "experiences." These are made possible by an impressive creative imagination, coupled with a dedication and integrity to his craft.

Indeed, Russell Crowe is truly committed to his work, even though he appears neglectful and unaffected by the bad press that is flaunted by the paparazzi or tabloid writers who condemn him for his "ungrateful" resentment of the adulation afforded him. Damning publicity aside, the upward momentum of Russell Crowe's career seems almost a given. He is an inspiration to students of acting who recognize and benefit from his solid professionalism, exemplified by both the subtlety and dynamism of his performances. The power of his performances transcends the imagery magnified on the motion picture screen.

And so we **return** to the question proffered earlier in this introduction: **Who is Russell Crowe?**

Russell Crowe is a contemporary talent not easy to categorize. Indeed he is the sum of many parts—a compilation of many who have come before him, those who have influenced him in his profession and others to whom he has become the heir apparent. Russell Crowe fits comfortably into the A-list of motion picture actors, the elite who are recognized both for their box office drawing power and their talent. Since his Oscar-winning turn as Maximus Decimus Meridius in *Gladiator*, Russell has continued to seek out new and daring challenges. He has been hailed as the later-day successor to the rebellious Marlon Brando, a hard-edged noir inheritor of Humphrey Bogart, a competent challenger to the comedic and dramatic complexities of Spencer Tracy and an adventurer/swashbuckler à la Errol Flynn. Critics have described him as each of these, most notably in *Romper Stomper, L.A. Confidential, A Beautiful Mind* and *Master and Commander: The Far Side of the World*. So it remains a frustrating task to try to fit him into a single mold.

Russell Crowe has expressed an arrogance exemplified by bad-boy behavior along his journey to film prominence. This attitude is perhaps explained by his early desire to achieve and maintain an independent identity.

aspiring to
be Elvis

ussell Crowe was not the product of a home life that would foster an attitude of rebellion. On the contrary, Russell Ira Crowe entered the world under the happiest of circumstances on April 7, 1964, born to Alex and Jocelyn Crowe of Strathmore Park, New Zealand. His ethnic background is Norwegian and Maori, and he takes great pride in his Maori heritage. Russell is one-sixteenth Maori and is registered on the Maori voting poll in New Zealand.

Geographically, New Zealand stands out from many other regions of the world. It is made up of two islands. The northern island, where Russell was born, is a pristine country landscape where sheep graze peacefully. However, New Zealand also has a darker side—it is an unstable landmass where geysers and the threat of sudden volcanic eruptions lurk under the surface. That same duality can be said to show the character and artistic temperament of Russell Crowe.

Russell was not born either in the green countryside or the uncertain terra firma of New Zealand. Rather, Strathmore Park is a suburb of Wellington, the country's capital and its primary port. Most of the city's 150,000 people choose to live there because of its agreeable climate and less rugged terrain.

At the time of Russell's birth, Alex and Jocelyn Crowe were employed as caterers for New Zealand's movie industry. It was steady but not terribly profitable work. The Crowes already had another son, Terry, with whom Russell shared a close, brotherly bond.

Russell's first interest was music, and family members often joked that it was because he was born the same year that

CROWE FAN FACT
Russell's nickname is "Rusty."

The Beatles hit it big with their highly publicized first North American appearance. His parents encouraged his musical ambitions by buying him a guitar when he was just six years old.

Russell also displayed an early interest in acting by frequently mimicking people, which sometimes led to some embarrassing moments for his parents when their son launched into unflattering imitations of their friends.

In 1970, the Crowes pulled up roots and moved to Sydney, Australia, where Alex and Jocelyn were offered jobs on a television series called *Spyforce*, which was directed by Jocelyn's godfather, Roger Mirams. It was a daring move for the family given the uncertainty of television, but if the show was successful, they expected to have guaranteed consistent employment for many years.

When not in school, Russell often accompanied his parents to the set, where he became fascinated by the make-believe of film production. His interest in motion pictures was further fostered by his grandfather, Stan Wemyss, who had worked as a cameraman during World War II and became renowned for his harrowing footage of battlefield combat.

Stan Wemyss operated a little film theater complete with studios in the basement of his house, and Russell visited constantly, marveling at his grandfather's work. Six-year-old Russell's first interest in the movie industry was *behind* the camera, not in front of it.

During the making of *Spyforce,* Jocelyn learned that the casting director was seeking a child to play a recurring role on the wartime series. She managed to persuade her godfather to give

Russell an audition. While Russell wasn't successful in winning the role, he was given the part of an orphan child, one of many who are rescued by the series star, Jack Thompson (who later went on to movie success in such films as *Star Wars: Episode II* and the Clint Eastwood-directed *Midnight in the Garden of Good and Evil*).

This brief TV experience with its single line of dialogue immediately hooked Russell on acting. With the support of his family, Russell went on auditions, seeking to land another TV role, but to no avail. He finally became discouraged in this ambition when at age 10 he lost a front tooth while playing rugby. He felt that his already limited opportunities were permanently halted owing to this "disfigurement."

At the time, Russell was enrolled at Sydney Boys High School where other than playing a guest part on the TV series *The Young Doctors*, he didn't put much emphasis on drama—except for schoolyard high jinks.

But Russell did not completely close the door on his creative passions. He embraced his love of music with fervor, though the stability of his life was once again compromised when Russell learned that the *Spyforce* series had closed production. The Crowe clan tried to resume their catering business for various movie companies, but that entailed frequent moves for the family. Finally, Alex announced that he and his family would move back to New Zealand. Russell was 14 when his father gave up the catering business completely and settled with his wife and sons in Auckland, where he found employment as manager of a pub called The Albion.

Russell enrolled at Auckland Grammar School, where he was not noted for his academic achievement.

This brief TV experience with its single line of dialogue immediately hooked Russell on acting.

Nor was Russell very popular socially. He still enjoyed sports, particularly rugby, but his athletic ability paled next to the skills of more talented players.

He'd developed a competitive streak that often didn't endear him to others. He didn't like to lose. His grandfather Stan's second wife remembered playing tennis with the 14-year-old once, and when she beat him, he threw his racket across the court in a rage. Russell had also begun to adopt a tough-guy attitude, smoking and hanging out with his older brother Terry and his cousins Martin and Jeff (both of whom later achieved their own celebrity status as champion cricket players).

> After only a year at Auckland Grammar School, it was suggested that Russell and Terry should be transferred to Mount Roskill Grammar School in the hope of bettering their academic future. In truth, this "recommendation" was made so the school wouldn't have to ask Russell to leave because of his poor school record.

It was as if Russell were having difficulty "finding himself." He hadn't succeeded as an actor, nor did he see much of a future as a professional rugby player. He certainly wasn't going to excel as an academic. Just what could he do?

The answer came one day when he was visiting his father's pub and had his first personal exposure to Tom Sharplin and the Cadillacs, one of New Zealand's most popular rock-and-roll bands. Russell was so impressed with the group that he went to their dressing room to talk with them—and left with a definite plan for his future.

He was going to be the next Elvis Presley.

chapter 2

Roq and Roll

With his ambitions now firmly set, Russell went about assembling his own rock band, which he named The Profile. It was during the band's genesis that Russell first displayed professional arrogance. He showed cocky and disrespectful behavior towards a competing band during a school assembly hall performance when both he and another band member rudely turned their backs on the stage—which resulted in the entire audience turning their backs on The Profile when it came their turn to play.

Russell was unaffected by their reception, and the group continued to play. Shortly afterwards, he decided to experiment with other musical stylings, including punk, and he briefly formed a band called Dave Deceit and the Interrogators (with himself naturally as "Dave"). At the same time he decided the only way to advance his musical ambitions was to drop out of school. At the age of 16, the only job Russell could find was selling insurance. He worked at this job for five months before his musical mentor Tom Sharplin hired him as a DJ for his new nightclub, King Creole's. Much to his parents' disapproval, Russell quickly quit his day job and, though just barely 17, went to work in a licensed establishment, working late hours spinning records.

Russell enjoyed his work—after all, it beat hustling insurance policies. But his dream was still to get his own band together and cut a record. He asked Sharplin for advice.

> But his dream was still to get his own band together and cut a record. He asked Sharplin for advice.

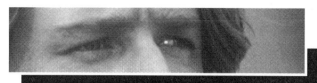

CROWE FAN FACT

One of the reasons Russell changed his name
was to disassociate himself from his famous
rugby-playing cousins, Martin and Jeff Crowe.

One of Sharplin's first suggestions was that Russell should
change his name, which he did—to Russ le Roq. Russell was
thrilled. He finally had a separate identity, one that was appro-
priate to his passion. Under Sharplin's tutelage, Russell further
built upon his Russ le Roq image by developing a 1950s-type
leather-jacketed appeal. He planned to build this image into a
complete alter ego, one who would strut his persona both
onstage and off.

In 1982, Sharplin arranged for Russell to record his first album,
even enlisting some of his own musicians to provide backup.
Russell composed a single called *I Just Want to be Like Marlon
Brando*, which was released by Ode Records. Marlon Brando
and Steve McQueen were among Russell's acting idols. The
record was not a chart-breaker, receiving only two local radio
airplays and selling just 500 copies. Alter ego Russ le Roq was
disappointed by the record's failure, but he was not discouraged.
Russell Crowe, however, was impatient and frustrated.

Fortunes began to pick up for Russell in 1983, when Ode
Records released his second single, *Pier 13*. He put together a
new three-piece backing band that he called Russ le Roq and the
Romantics, their apparel inspired by the onstage dress of Tom
Sharplin and the Cadillacs. Then he set about promoting the
band with blatant PR that bordered on arrogance. He reasoned
that until he had proper management, he had to create his own
publicity, which he did aggressively.

He created a fictional fan club for the group for which he composed a newsletter providing updates on the band's activities.

Then he built up his own rebel image, proclaiming on the liner notes of a new recording that the contents were not "rock and roll" but "*Roq* and roll." He was rude to his fans, even the females. A friend later explained this behavior by saying that Russell was trying to create an "ultra-machismo" reputation among his "mates." Russell's reasoning was simply that it was better to have an image of arrogance than no image at all.

Despite his aggressive and imaginative efforts, Russell could not make a living from his music, and he was forced to take day jobs to survive. It was humbling for a man with such an immensely driven nature to work as a bingo caller—he occasionally gave vent to his frustration by insulting the players.

Yet Russ le Roq and the Romantics continued to crank out tunes. Russell himself wrote *St. Kilda* ("Le Music"), and there were other songs, including *Never Let Ya Slide*, *Fire* and *Shattered Glass*. Each one apparently sounded a resounding death knell for Russell's rock-and-roll aspirations.

Undeterred, in 1984 Russell invested his royalties into opening his own nightclub, which he called The Venue. His club was in a poor location and wasn't licensed to sell alcohol, but Russell was less concerned with those factors than with providing the music that he believed would draw in patrons. Within nine months, The Venue closed—a valiant but failed enterprise.

Yet in one respect Russell benefited from his loss, if only creatively. He teamed up with one of his club's frequent musicians, a guitarist named Dean Cochran from the band Third Wave, and while Dean's musical preferences were best exemplified by the group AC/DC, he and Russell combined their talents to put together a band called Roman Antix.

> Despite his aggressive and imaginative efforts, Russell could not make a living from his music, and he was forced to take day jobs to survive.

Within a year, after honing and meshing their divergent skills on club dates, Roman Antix released its first album, *What's the Difference*. Still, even after it was decided to make a change within the group, the prospects of this new band appeared to Russell as bleak as his other attempts at rock-and-roll stardom.

Russell was 18. Perhaps he should once again seek a different career direction. He was ambitious, so was impatient and anxious to move on to tomorrow.

chapter 3

rocky horror

Russell

I t was 1986.

Russell was as excited as he'd been in a long time. An opportunity had presented itself that might allow him to exploit both his musical talent and satisfy his long-held acting ambitions.

The hugely successful *The Rocky Horror Picture Show* (lensed for the movie screen in 1975) was having success as a stage musical under the title *The Rocky Horror Show*. Theater producers Wilton Morley and Peter Davis were planning to stage the production in New Zealand and were looking for actors.

Russell didn't have to audition for a part in the show. Morley and Davis saw him playing in a band in Auckland and immediately hired him. As Peter Davis later said, "You could say 'a star was born'. We 'discovered' a few people along the way and helped launch their careers, but Russell is probably the most famous."

Russell was awarded two roles: Dr. Everett von Scott, an elderly gentleman confined to a wheelchair, and the brief part of Eddie, who was played onscreen by '70s singer Meat Loaf, a simple part that required Russell to come onstage, sing a song, then get murdered.

It was the part of 65-year-old Dr. von Scott that intrigued the 19-year-old. Not only was it the larger role; it also was a challenge that would test whatever talent he possessed as an actor. If he could pull it off, he thought he would again consider acting as a career.

Russell continued to call himself Russ le Roq during the play's five-month run in an attempt to establish his new, preferred identity. The play was enormously successful, and Russ la Roq received recognition among the sell-out audiences for his flamboyant onstage presence.

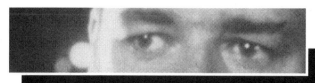

CROWE FAN FACT

According to a 2003 survey by the Beverly Hills Institute for Aesthetic and Reconstructive Surgery in Los Angeles, Russell Crowe has the best chin among male celebrities.

Following the New Zealand run of the play, Russell tried to see if he could once more make a go of it with his band Roman Antix, but again the band was not successful. At that point, he decided to again take his chances with *The Rocky Horror Show* and rejoined the company in Australia. He hoped to expand his own opportunities by taking on the key role of Dr. Frank-N-Furter, portrayed most notoriously onscreen by Tim Curry.

Russell won the part and went about creating a characterization decidedly different from Tim Curry's version of the role. The part was a double-edged sword for Russell. It gave him a chance to exaggerate his musical and acting abilities into high camp. But he was so convincing that rumors began to circulate regarding his sexual orientation.

One memorable moment occurred when a man in the audience shouted a compliment to Russell regarding his fishnet-stockinged legs. Russell snapped out of character quickly to respond: "You'd never make it as a transvestite because there isn't enough lipstick in the world to cover your big mouth."

Russell managed to supplement his downtime earnings from *The Rocky Horror Show* with local television commercials and short films. He also refused to surrender his passion for performing rock-and-roll music.

The so-called "Australian Invasion" began during the 1980s. Suddenly, two of the most popular leading men in movies were Paul Hogan and Mel Gibson. Aussie musical talents were prominently represented by Rick Springfield (*Jesse's Girl*) and the duo Air Supply, whose song *The One That You Love* topped the charts in 1980. Other Australian groups of note included Men at Work (*Who Can It Be Now*) and the Little River Band (*Lonesome Loser*). The time seemed right for Russell Crowe to proceed with his own career plans.

He stayed with *The Rocky Horror Show* until 1988, performing a total of 416 shows. When the show's run ended, he stayed in Sydney. Until he could land another acting role, he returned to taking on odd jobs, including working as a waiter and washing cars. On some occasions he even "sang for his supper" by busking. He lived in a cheap, rented room that cost him $50 a week and allowed himself $3.50 a day spending money, subsisting on cigarettes and fried rice.

These were **difficult days** for Russell, but he **never stopped believing** in himself.

He continued auditioning for plays, hoping to pursue a career in the theater. He appeared in a short film produced by the Seventh Day Adventist church called *A Very Special Reason*, where Russell played a farm worker who decides to join the Christian group.

He did get some theatrical work, though. He auditioned for and won the role of Mickey in Willy Russell's *Blood Brothers*, which told the story of twins separated at birth who rediscover each other later in life. Apparently, there was animosity between Russell and his theatrically trained co-star Peter Cousens. Their personal conflict was revealed almost nightly during a scene in which Russell threw a pistol across the stage after shooting Cousens. Russell's pitch usually struck his co-star's prone body with painful and often precise accuracy. Finally, Cousens could no longer stand the abuse and confronted Russell. Russell reacted aggressively by throwing a punch, but he was grabbed by others in the dressing room. Russell broke free and gave Cousens a head-butt.

"The bastard had broken my nose!" Cousens recalled a few years later.

When Russell refused to comply with director Danny Hill's demand for a mutual apology, Crowe was fired.

> **Russell suffered a deep personal blow in 1988 when his beloved grandfather, Stan, passed away of cancer at the age of 72. Russell was so distraught that his grandmother advised him not to fly back to New Zealand for the funeral.**

Once more, Russell had to consider his professional options. He could apply at Sydney's National Institute of Dramatic Arts (NIDA), which boasted Mel Gibson as an alumnus. But, truthfully, Russell was afraid. As he later explained, "There's a lot more bodies on the roadside from going to NIDA than there are stars." He felt that going there had destroyed many people's talents and dreams and that he probably would become one of that failed group.

Russell and Dean Cochran instead chose to press forward with their rock-and-roll aspirations until the next acting opportunity presented itself. Unfortunately, their style of music was not in sync with what was then the vogue, which included the enormously popular but short-lived New Kids on the Block. Musical tastes change more quickly than any other popular art form, including cinema. It was not from lack of trying that Russell did not find success in the music world.

Fortunately, his frustrating musical excursions brought him back to acting.

chapter 4

Romping onto the Big Screen

ussell began appearing regularly on Australian television, showing up on such popular programs as the courtroom drama *Rafferty's Rules* and playing four times on the daytime soap opera *Neighbours*. Russell later admitted that the main reason he appeared in the latter series was to get close to the star, Kylie Minogue, who later achieved international success as a singer. In 1988, he had his own short-lived police series, *Living with the Law,* in which he played Gary Harding.

While none of this work gave Russell artistic satisfaction, he was able to earn good money.

> While none of this work gave Russell artistic satisfaction, he was able to earn good money.

More importantly, it brought him to the attention of Sydney-based agents Bedford and Pearce—as well as director George Ogilvie, who had helmed the 1985 Mel Gibson-starring blockbuster *Mad Max Beyond Thunderdome*. Ogilvie had Crowe in mind for a starring role in his upcoming movie, *The Crossing*.

Before Russell began work on that production, however, one of Ogilvie's film students, Steve Wallace, was interested in casting him in a small part in his movie *Prisoners of the Sun*. Written by Denis Whitburn and Brian A. Williams, the film is based on the true story of an Australian military lawyer delegated to prosecute Japanese war criminals on the island of Ambon. Australian actor Bryan Brown, who had starred in the popular American movies *F/X* (1986), *Gorillas in the Mist* (1988) and *Cocktail* (1988), played the lead role of Captain Cooper, while Russell was assigned the part of Lt. Corbett,

Cooper's assistant counsel in the trial investigations. Russell admitted that playing the subordinate part didn't give him much challenge, although he said that he learned a lot working alongside Bryan Brown.

The film did quite well in Australia, where it went under the title *Blood Oath*. The picture received its North American release in 1991, where unfortunately it did not attract a wide audience perhaps because of its grim subject matter or because almost half of the film takes place in a courtroom. More probable, though, is that it was lost in the shuffle, competing against such summer blockbusters as *Terminator 2*.

Russell was disappointed that his movie debut did not make more of an impact in the U.S., but he was pleased with the final product. Even though his part was comparatively small, the 10-week shoot proved an enjoyable one, and he decided to concentrate his efforts on obtaining more movie work.

His next film, *The Crossing*, provided Russell with a much more substantial role as Johnny, a farm boy involved in a romantic triangle with Sam (Robert Mammone) and Meg (Danielle Spencer). Set in a country town over a 24-hour period during the mid-1960s, the movie explores the relationship of three childhood friends that ultimately culminates in a tragic resolution at the town's railroad crossing.

Director George Ogilvie initially had second thoughts concerning his decision to cast Russell in the film. Apparently, he detected a competitive arrogance in the actor that could cause problems during the production. To Ogilvie's relief Russell proved himself a total professional during the making of the movie. He embraced co-stars Mammone and Spencer as friends, and their chemistry came through on the screen. Ogilvie discerned a raw talent in Russell, perfect for the character as he perceived him and did not restrict the actor with rigid direction, allowing Russell's natural dramatic instincts to have free reign in many of the film's more powerful scenes.

"He let me go wild because he trusted me," Russell said.

As Ogilvie later remarked, "Russell Crowe is the sort of actor you watch work and have no idea what he will do next."

He further explained that Russell was right for the part of Johnny, because the character possesses the same duality that is inherent in the actor. Both Johnny and Russell have a physical explosiveness while being basically gentle souls. Perhaps nowhere is Russell's sensitivity more apparent than in a scene early in the picture where his character makes love to Meg. It was an understandably difficult sequence for the two relatively inexperienced actors, but what emerges onscreen is neither awkward nor embarrassing.

The Crossing (1990)

His work on *The Crossing* cemented Russell's decision to choose film work over the stage. He found acting for the camera exhilarating, and he seemed to have a natural ability. He could prepare a scene for hours and then step before the cameras and deliver a spontaneous, believable performance.

The success of *The Crossing* paid dividends for Russell Crowe, both professionally and personally. He was awarded with critical praise and an Australian Film Institute nomination in 1990 for his performance.

Russell's participation in the movie was the basis for a strong relationship with co-star Danielle Spencer, who he married 13 years later. She was 20, blonde and appealed to Russell in every way. Perhaps it was their passionate love scene that proved the impetus for their eventual romance—"eventual" because at the time Danielle was involved in another relationship, and Russell was preoccupied with his burgeoning career.

The actor's one obvious physical imperfection was a broken front tooth from his long-ago rugby mishap. Ogilvie believed that close-ups of Russell that exposed his broken tooth would prove a distraction to the audience. Surprising to Ogilvie, the dental flaw was not a big concern to Russell despite the fact he was standing at the threshold of motion-picture recognition. Russell believed that the power of his acting would overcome any cosmetic imperfection. He displayed stubbornness, arrogance and conceit and held strong to his commitment to his chosen craft, ignoring what he considered a side issue. When Ogilvie argued that the character of Johnny had no reason to have a broken tooth and sweetened the deal by offering to foot the bill, Russell finally consented to have his tooth repaired.

Russell's next film, *Proof*, had its genesis when a movie directorial hopeful named Jocelyn Moorhouse came across a story concerning a blind photographer who snaps photographs that he later asks others to describe for him. After three years of script rewrites, Moorhouse had finally prepared a screenplay that she could present to various funding organizations, eventually receiving the financial support of both the Australian Film Commission and Film Victoria. Producer Lynda House was instantly attracted to the story and production for the picture was quickly underway, with a budget of $1.1 million.

Twenty-three-year-old Russell Crowe read the script and was immediately intrigued. He was hired for the role of Andy, a young dishwasher who befriends the lead character, the blind photographer Martin, and helps him interpret his photographs. His co-stars were the Nigerian-born Hugo Weaving (Martin), who had immigrated to Australia as a teenager and was a graduate of the Australian Film Institute, and Genevieve Picot, who played Celia, Martin's vindictive housekeeper.

In the film, which echoes Joseph Losey's 1963 masterpiece *The Servant*, Martin, who has been blind since birth, distrusts people and lives vicariously through his photography. He meets and becomes friendly with Andy, whose kindness and sincerity leads to a friendship between the two. Martin asks Andy to describe his photographs for him. Complications arise when Martin's housekeeper Celia plots revenge at Martin's constant spurning of her affections by seducing Andy in order to destroy the two men's friendship.

Michael Upchurch from the ***Seattle Times*** singled out Russell's performance by summarizing, "It's Crowe who holds ***Proof*** together."

Proof received generally positive acknowledgment from critics, including Michael Upchurch from the *Seattle Times* who singled out Russell's performance by summarizing, "It's Crowe who holds *Proof* together."

Washington Post writer Rita Kempley noted, "It's the hubris that first attracts Crowe's Everyman Andy. Crowe is indigenous to the project, a Down Underling whose sunny ordinariness helps liberate Martin."

> Although it was a small film, **Proof** was a contender at the prestigious Cannes Film Festival in 1991, where it won director Jocelyn Moorhouse the Golden Camera Award. Russell Crowe also emerged a winner when he was awarded the award for Best Supporting Actor by the Australian Film Institute.

That same year, he was offered a small but important role in the six-part Australian miniseries *Brides of Christ*, which starred Brenda Fricker and Naomi Watts and was directed by Ken Cameron. The program, which aired in North America on A&E, tells the story of teachers and students at a convent school in 1960s Australia in a time of religious and social change.

Russell plays Dominic Maloney, who becomes the love interest of one of his female students at the school. The young woman has begun to question the teachings of the Catholic Church while at the same time discovering her own sexuality. Their romance ends abruptly with the onset of the Vietnam War. Russell

> Russell Crowe also emerged a winner when he was awarded the award for Best Supporting Actor by the Australian Film Institute.

was most effective in the role and was particularly pleased to be able to both sing and play the guitar in the film. The miniseries first aired in Australia on September 4, 1991, and garnered huge audience ratings, recapturing this success when it played in North America in 1993.

It was a heady time for Russell, and he occasionally capitalized on his success by applauding his own accomplishments. One night it was reported by his bed companion that he even cheered on his own prowess as a lover, chanting, "Go Russ, go!"

Modesty has never been a quality associated with Russell Crowe. Yet there remained in him the desire to establish a permanent romantic relationship, and after he returned from Cannes, he looked up Danielle Spencer and asked her out to dinner. Danielle had made some impressive inroads with her own acting career, having completed work on the feature *What the Moon Saw* and beginning work on a TV movie. More importantly, she had broken up with her boyfriend. She accepted Russell's dinner invitation and that evening proved to be the start of Russell's first serious romantic involvement.

"I played around a lot, you know?" he later said. "But not until I met Danielle did I know what a real relationship could be."

He also discovered what **true talent** was when he signed to **play opposite** the distinguished **Anthony Hopkins** in

Spotswood.

Directed by Mark Joffe, *Spotswood* is an odd film that, while billed as a comedy, is really quite humorless. Its main attraction is the participation of Anthony Hopkins, who agreed to the movie soon after garnering the Best Actor Academy Award for his role as the demonic Dr. Hannibal Lector in *Silence of the Lambs* (1991). Russell was billed down the cast list as Kim Barry, a moccasin factory employee who, in his desire to gain favor with efficiency expert Errol Wallace (Hopkins), steals company documents that expose the truth about the factory.

Even though the role was small, Russell enjoyed the part and later referred to Kim as "a wonderful little character." Russell even added a bit of self-assessment: "He's a parody of ambition—or myself when I was a little younger. He thinks he's super-cool, but the bottom line is that he's not."

> **Hopkins was complimentary of his co-star's work, saying, "He's a very fine actor, and I was impressed with his determination. He's very prepared, quite intense and knows exactly what to do."**

Certainly Russell picked up acting tips from Anthony Hopkins à la Hannibal Lecter, and put these to valuable effect in his next film, an uncompromising look at the bigotry and violence still prevalent on the streets of Sydney and Melbourne. The movie was called *Romper Stomper* and could best be compared to Stanley Kubrick's classic *A Clockwork Orange*. Russell, who vigorously campaigned for the lead role in the Geoffrey Wright-directed movie, later admitted to being both excited yet fearful at playing such a vile character.

"He was extreme," said Russell.

Initially another actor was set for the role, but Russell was so desperate to play the part that he called up director Wright virtually every day telling him that *he* was the better man to play Hando. Wright had to tell Russell that there was no way

Initially another actor was set for the role, but Russell was so desperate to play the part that he called up director Wright virtually every day telling him that *he* was the better man to play Hando.

Romper Stomper (1992)

he could release the other actor from the commitment. Russell was persistent—until finally Wright called up Russell and told him, "You've got the part."

What clinched the deal for Russell had less to do with his ability than with the fact that he looked more menacing with a razor-shaved head than the fellow originally cast. But Wright was further convinced he'd made the correct choice when he watched *Proof*, later remarking, "Russell was the most menacing gentle dishwasher I'd ever seen."

Russell wasn't unfamiliar with racism. He remembered visiting one of the pubs his father managed and witnessing violent clashes of bigotry between cultures far removed from simple black and white. He had personally experienced bigotry in New Zealand for being white.

To help Russell prepare for the part of the skinhead leader, Wright provided him with copies of *Mein Kampf* and *The History of the Third Reich*. Russell became so fascinated by the psychology of pure evil that he picked up other books dealing with aberrant behavior, such as *Murder in the 20th Century* and *The History of the Criminal Mind*.

To get in shape physically to play the intimidating bully, Russell worked out in a gym with an instructor/motivator who prompted Russell's bench presses with such words of encouragement as: "You hate…"

He even met with members of a skinhead gang to observe their mannerisms and characteristics. He picked up details such as the type of clothing they generally favored. He also talked with them, trying to discover what made them tick. Finally, after delving as deeply as he cared to go into the psychology of violence and hate, he stepped before the cameras—and a monster named Hando emerged.

From the moment Hando first appears onscreen, his hate is evident. He accosts a young Vietnamese skateboarder with the accusation "This is not your country" before giving the girl a vicious beating. In the film, Hando and his skinhead gang rebel against the influx of Asians immigrating to Australia. Hando in particular is determined to stop this change in the population mix and finds his motivation in Nazi propaganda. Finally, the two cultures clash when the skinheads attack a group of Vietnamese planning to purchase their favorite bar, leading to a bloody retaliation when the Asians raid the warehouse where the skinheads have made their home and base. Violence begets violence, and at the picture's end Hando is killed by his best friend Davey as Hando attempts to murder his girlfriend on the beach. Ironically, this act is witnessed by a departing busload of Japanese tourists.

The entire movie was shot in just 28 days, and upon its release in 1992, critical reaction to the film was as extreme as the characters in the movie. Some called it an unregenerate exercise in excess, while others regarded it as a contemporary masterpiece. One reviewer of the former category was so outraged that he suggested the film negative should be burned.

Perhaps Jeff Shannon of the *Seattle Times* offered the most perceptive observation when he concluded his review of the picture by saying, "It [*Romper Stomper*] demands to be responded to, for the simple reason that, if this film were to be reviewed by a superior alien race, they would instantly deem humans primitive and unworthy of survival."

Russell complimented George Wright for having the courage to make the film in the first place, "If you just choose to ignore them, you only make them more intriguing."

Still, the film produced a storm of controversy concerning excessive violence masquerading as entertainment, and director Wright was accused of glamorizing fascism. Local politicians in the film's setting, Melbourne, called for a boycott of the movie, and Australian Prime Minister Paul Keating called the film "morally bankrupt."

But the high-profile criticism produced the opposite effect. *Romper Stomper* broke box office records with some cinemas running extra showings just to keep up with public demand. The success of *Romper Stomper* was gratifying to Russell, as he'd put a lot of hard work into it. At the same time he was glad that filming had finished and he could shed himself of Hando.

Russell's frightening but incisive portrayal of a man of rage earned him a series of awards, culminating in his receiving the Australian Film Institute's Best Actor Award in 1992.

Romper Stomper (1992)

"Russell deserved the award," remarked George Wright, "because he took it to the max."

Rather than taking a much-needed break following the intense demands of *Romper Stomper*, Russell quickly went back to work, researching the role of horse trainer East Driscoll for *Hammers over the Anvil*. He prepared for the part by enduring such discomforts as sleeping in a car parked outside a stable, eating and sleeping with horses and mastering horseback riding after many hours of strenuous practice.

> In the picture, Russell was billed second beneath actress Charlotte Rampling, a popular actress of the '70s and '80s whose career ran the gamut from a guest role in TV's campy *The Avengers* series to film parts opposite Paul Newman, Robert Mitchum and Sean Connery. Rampling's career had slid a little by this time, but she was still an established name.

Yet it is East Driscoll who provides the attraction for the story, playing a role much like Robert Redford's in the 1998 film *The Horse Whisperer*. East is a solitary man who finds comfort and companionship with his horses. Later, he begins an affair with Grace McAlister (Rampling), who is the wife of the richest and most prominent man in the community. Their relationship eventually results in tragedy when Grace decides to end their liaison, and East Driscoll is critically injured in a fall from one of his beloved horses. Grace must make the difficult choice between staying with her husband or caring for Driscoll.

Hammers Over the Anvil is based on a story by Alan Marshall (played in the film by Alexander Outhred) that had its genesis in Marshall's own childhood recollections. It is a simple, gentle film that unfortunately did not receive a theatrical release in North

America, going immediately to video. Russell was pleased with the movie, particularly since he was given the opportunity to display his musical ability. In the film he both plays the guitar and sings a love ballad.

After *Hammers Over the Anvil*, Russell's career took a turn—to comedy. Director David Elfick had produced a number of Australian features, including *Starstruck* and *Undercover*. He'd already seen Russell's work in *Proof* and *Romper Stomper* and was enormously impressed with the actor's talent. Elfick wanted to cast Russell in his upcoming comedy *Love in Limbo*. Even though his name would be billed down the cast list, Russell was thrilled at the chance to finally play in a comedy and even provided character suggestions to Elfick, who readily complied.

In the film, Russell plays against type as Arthur Baskin, a 21-year-old clothing factory warehouse supervisor who decides to achieve his manhood by joining his buddies Barry and Ken on a road trip to a notorious brothel where the three hope to lose their virginity. To add a personal dimension to the role, Russell decided to employ a Welsh accent he remembered being effectively used by Anthony Hopkins in *Spotswood*. Determined to perfect the correct vocal qualities, he paid out of pocket for a two-week stay in a small town in Wales where he absorbed the rhythm of speech of the locals.

Russell's dedication carried onto the set, where he went, even on days when he was not working, to climb into wardrobe and just sit before a mirror staring at his own reflection. While some of the crew thought he was eccentric if not vain, David Elfick completely understood Russell's motivation.

"Russell has tremendous focus when doing a part," he explained.

> Russell was thrilled at the chance to finally play in a comedy and even provided character suggestions to Elfick, who readily complied.

33

Russell himself had great enthusiasm for the role, saying, "It was the first time I got to go haywire on the screen."

Unfortunately, because *Love in Limbo* (also known as *Just One Night*) was a "little" film, it did poor business in Australia when it was released in 1993 and did not even make it into the North American market.

The film had been a location shoot, which meant a separation from Danielle Spencer. Instead of rushing into another picture, once *Love in Limbo* wrapped, Russell decided to take some time out to return to his music. To him music was soul cleansing, and he needed to "reinvigorate" himself after the physical and emotional demands of his heavy work schedule.

> "I was feeling the pressure from all the films I was doing at the time," Russell said. "I needed to get back to what I used to do, with the music."

Russell re-teamed with his musical colleague Dean Cochran and, together with three other musicians, put together a band known as 30 Odd Foot of Grunts (TOFOG). Their gigs were not extraordinary. They played mainly pub bookings, but Russell found each experience exhilarating.

"Playing with a band is not much different from acting in a movie," he explained. "In fact, it's a great way to learn how to maneuver an audience."

It wasn't long before Russell was called back before the movie cameras. Like *Hammers over the Anvil*, *The Silver Brumby* appealed to Russell because of its location shooting on rugged landscape. A large part of the picture was filmed in the mountains of Victoria, Australia. An extra incentive to the actor was that he would again be working with horses, of which he had become very fond. He was also allowed to do his own stunts, including one potentially treacherous action that required him to wade into a stream to rescue a struggling calf, then carry it ashore in his arms.

> "I had maybe a half dozen lines of dialogue," Russell said of his character. "It wasn't like making a film—it was like experiencing a whole different lifestyle."

Based on the classic children's novel by Elyne Mitchell, *The Silver Brumby* (or *The Silver Stallion*) tells the story of Thowra, a wild stallion that seeks to survive man and nature in the wilderness of the Australian mountains. According to legend, the Silver Brumby can never be tamed, even though The Man (Crowe) is determined to capture the horse to use for breeding stock. The film ends on a mystical note, when Thowra leaps from a cliff rather than be caught, leaving the audience to wonder whether the local residents' stories of a "ghost horse" are indeed real or the figments of their imagination—and whether perhaps Thowra still lives.

Despite the ambiguity of its ending, *The Silver Brumby* is

"Playing with a band is not much different from acting in a movie," he explained. "In fact, it's a great way to learn how to maneuver an audience."

excellent family viewing and remains one of Russell's favorite films for exactly that reason.

"It's a magical story, and I'd love some 25-year-old to come up to me one day and say, 'I saw you in that film when I was a kid,'" he said.

The Silver Brumby was the second time Russell fell in love on a movie location. This time his affections were directed towards co-star Coolie, his character's faithful canine companion. The trainer allowed Russell to take the dog home during shooting so that the two could develop a camaraderie, which they did. When the film wrapped, Russell wanted very much to keep the dog, but the owner refused. Later, however, the actor was given one of Coolie's pups, Chasen.

Russell's next assignment took him away from movies onto the stage when he was asked to participate in *The Official Tribute to the Blue Brothers*, a musical homage to the Dan Aykroyd–John Belushi duo that was to be performed at Sydney's Metro Theatre.

Prior to this performance Russell was summoned to America to consider movie offers. He was beginning to find the Australian film industry too small for his aspirations and felt that the roles he was offered lacked variety. With the support of his Australian agent, Shirley Pearce,

He was beginning to find the Australian film industry too small for his aspirations and felt that the roles he was offered lacked variety.

Russell decided to try his luck in Hollywood. One of the first parts he was offered was a supporting role in the *Shawshank Redemption*. Russell perused the script, which he liked, but then offered some observations on why he should play the role, later discovering that this self-promotion was not Hollywood "etiquette."

Russell arrived in L.A. already under scrutiny for his controversial performance in *Romper Stomper*. He made the round of guest appearances on American TV programs, where he made some trenchant comments about Los Angeles that failed to endear him to prospective movie employers.

It is doubtful that Russell gave much thought to blowing his "big chance" in America. He knew there would be other offers. Besides, he was homesick for Sydney after spending so much time away on various film locations. He'd also enjoyed precious little time with Danielle and wanted to make it up to her. He realized that despite all the exciting things that were happening for him, he really wasn't enjoying life as much as he should.

He was, however, still committed to the Blues Brothers tribute and was looking forward to his musical stage role as Jake Blues.

But then—after only one performance—Russell had to remove himself from *The Official Tribute to the Blues Brothers* when he developed a throat problem. His doctors prescribed a week of rest, after which he could return to the show. Sadly, the promoter preferred to re-cast the part rather than wait for Russell to recover. Losing the part was traumatic for Russell, who started to fear that his voice might not have the strength for the singing work he still desired.

His illness required that he finally stop and rest for a while. He lazed around for two months until his strength returned then set about getting himself back in shape with regular workouts at the gym. He played with his band and worked out new musical arrangements. He also used this period to re-establish his relationship with the ever-patient Danielle.

> Russell once more decided to try his luck in Hollywood. As he explained it, "I'd gotten all the recognition I could get [in Australia]. I suddenly had to look overseas and look at expanding where I was going to work."

The actor realized that his best chance for success in the competitive movie community was to find himself an agent. He signed with International Creative Management (ICM), a firm that represented such strong film talents as Charlton Heston, Paul Newman, Meg Ryan, and fellow Aussie Mel Gibson. However, he quickly discovered that no matter how far his star had risen in Australia, he remained little known in the United States. He eventually managed to land work—not in a multimillion-dollar Hollywood blockbuster but rather in a low-budget feature called *For the Moment*, shot in Manitoba, Canada.

For the most part, Canadian films are financed by government subsidies (tax dollars). To give their productions international appeal while still watching the budget, Canadian producers cast their movies either with faded actors still of name value or up-and-coming potential stars who have already succeeded in their debuts but can be hired at a bargain price. Russell certainly fit into the latter category, and he accepted the Canadian assignment.

> The actor realized that his best chance for success in the competitive movie community was to find himself an agent.

For the Moment provided Russell with his first starring role since *Romper Stomper*. He played the part

For the Moment (1993)

of Lachlan, a conceited Australian who arrives at a flight training school in Manitoba during World War II to earn his wings as a combat pilot. Besides schooling alongside other would-be pilots, Lachlan meets and interacts with locals who live in the community outside the base.

> Russell always admitted to a fear of flying, and so he found the role especially challenging. At the same time, he had become discouraged and unsure about his career. He lamented his feelings to Danielle prior to leaving for Manitoba, but by the time he arrived in the Canadian Prairies, he was once more filled with optimism and enthusiasm.

Manitoba-born Aaron Kim Johnston wrote, produced and directed the project. Johnson's previous work included two well-received local productions: *Heartland* and *The Last Winter*. *For the Moment* was intended as a tribute to the pilots who volunteered for potentially suicidal air combat missions. Since the budget did not allow for extensive aerial sequences, Johnson instead decided to focus his film on the romances of these men, particularly Lachlan, who becomes involved in an adulterous affair with a local girl whose husband is overseas fighting for his country. Russell's love interest was played by Christianne Hirt, who is perhaps best known for her work on the television series *Lonesome Dove*.

Russell always admitted to a fear of flying, and so he found the role especially challenging.

For the Moment (1993)

CROWE FAN FACT

Russell's father in the film *The Sum of Us* was played by Jack Thompson, the star of the *Spyforce* series, for which Russell's parents had provided catering services. Jack Thompson will also play the role of Nicole Kidman's widowed father, Holland, in Russell's upcoming film *Eucalyptus*.

The film was well received by critics when it was released in 1993, but its slow pacing made it unpopular with audiences used to the explosions and pyrotechnics of most contemporary action films. Russell was awarded favorable praise for his performance with *Variety* saying that the actor delivered a "stardom-in-the-making lead performance." This film certainly didn't impede the upward momentum of his career.

His agent in Hollywood presented him with an offer to star opposite Jennifer Beals, who had scored a hit in the 1983 movie *Flashdance*, in a production called *Red Rain*. The film, in which Russell played an archeology professor, appealed to Russell because of his co-star and the Italian shooting location.

Then, just two weeks into production, the film was cancelled when the producers failed to pay their bills. Events happened so quickly that both Russell and Beals were hurried from their hotel rooms because the police were on their way to vacate the cast and crew.

Fortunately, Russell's career was on such a roll that after a brief stopover in Los Angeles, he was summoned back to Sydney to work on a film that almost equaled *Romper Stomper* in its controversial subject matter.

The Sum of Us, based on a play by David Stevens, explores a father/son dynamic in which each man is looking for a perfect partner. The son, Jeff Mitchell played by Russell, is gay. Russell claimed the script, co-written by the play's award-winning author, was the best he'd ever read, and he embraced the idea of playing a character who questions his own sexuality. What particularly appealed to Russell about doing a gay part was that, unlike many countries that are accepting of homosexuality, Australia regards itself as a masculine nation where the subject of homosexuality is practically taboo.

Russell's friends advised him against accepting the role, but from the moment he first heard of the project, he actively pursued the

The Sum of Us (1994)

role. It was suggested to him that he was on the brink of major stardom, and if he played the part convincingly, it might hurt his chances in Hollywood.

Russell has explained that he wanted to play the part of Jeff because he wanted to see if he could convincingly play a gay character. But he also looked beyond the "shocking" homosexual aspect of the film and saw a story, both funny and touching, that explored the relationship between a widowed father and his son.

The film is an affecting production, and Russell delivers a convincing performance that culminates in a fairly explicit homosexual love scene between Russell and co-star John Polson, who had earlier worked with Russell in *Blood Oath*.

Not surprisingly, the movie proved a troubled shoot, and at one point, a beer company hired to supply refreshments to the cast and crew refused to deliver to the set because of the movie's gay theme.

When *The Sum of Us* was released in Australia in 1994, it was greeted with a storm of critical controversy, but the publicity also helped to heighten the film's box office potency. It also did surprisingly well in the North American market, earning substantial profits both in the United States and Canada. Perhaps the one drawback to the film's commercial success and Russell's own performance was that rumors began to circulate that Russell Crowe himself might be gay.

As he explained it, "If I were indeed homosexual, I'd be a 'screaming queen'—that's where the fun is."

In fact, homosexual groups began to look upon him as one of their own.

Russell maintained an indifferent, if not amused attitude towards these rumors. As he explained it, "If I were indeed homosexual, I'd be a 'screaming queen'—that's where the fun is." The actor's humorous comments masked the frustration he was experiencing over still not having established himself in the Hollywood market. However, his fortunes were soon to turn.

a hot property in
Hollywood

The *Quick and the Dead* was an off-beat western co-produced by and starring Sharon Stone, who had just scored a big hit opposite Michael Douglas in the 1992 thriller *Basic Instinct*. Stone is an actress known as much for her intelligence (she reportedly possesses an IQ of 154) as for her striking blonde beauty, and based on the success of *Basic Instinct*, she decided to go into production on her own. She lined up a top-notch cast for her $35-million feature, including Gene Hackman for the role of villainous town boss John Herod, who holds annual shoot-to-kill contests, and an up-and-coming 19-year-old actor, Leonard DiCaprio, to play Herod's cocky son, referred to in the picture simply as "The Kid."

Other parts were played by such strong supporting actors as Roberts Blossom, Kevin Conway and, most notably, Lance Henriksen as the cool-headed gunfighter Ace Hanlon. Sharon's choice for director was a unique one, given the genre. After a list of 40 potential directors was submitted to her, she typed in only one name—Samuel Raimi.

Sam Raimi had achieved notoriety as the director of the incredibly violent *Evil Dead* films and hardly seemed to fit into cowboy boots with the same ease as John Ford, Burt Kennedy—or even Sam Peckinpah! But Sharon wanted the approach to her western to be individual and stylized, and Raimi seemed the perfect choice.

There was one more casting decision that Sharon felt was imperative to the success of the movie—the role of Cort, the former gunman who spends most of the movie suffering under the sadistic abuse of Gene Hackman. Sharon could

The Quick and the Dead (1995)

have decided on a "name" actor, but she immediately set her sights on Russell Crowe.

Tristar Pictures, the company financing the film, did not approve of Sharon's decision to use Russell because he was not potent box office, and he was Australian. Their casting suggestion was the Irish-born Liam Neeson, who had previously worked with Raimi in the 1990 film *Darkman*. Fortunately, Sharon had enough clout because of the $100 million-plus Tristar Pictures had earned from *Basic Instinct* to flex her muscles and demand the casting of Russell Crowe.

As she explained it, "When I saw *Romper Stomper*, I thought Russell was not only charismatic, attractive and talented, but also fearless." She also believed that Russell would not be intimidated by her status as a star screen player.

Which turned out to be the case. Russell was focused on achieving his own success in Hollywood after many failed attempts. He and Sharon worked well together, and the only difficulty he encountered was learning to master the intricacies of handling a gun. Russell had never fired a gun in his life, but in the film he was expected to perform all the gunslinger gymnastics of his character, including quick-draw twirling, as well as outdrawing his nemesis Hackman, who in real life had a reputation for being a very adept gun handler.

He and Sharon worked well together, and the only difficulty he encountered was learning to master the intricacies of handling a gun.

Russell went to a practice range in Tucson, Arizona, where he worked out daily with sheriff's deputies. His dedication was such that within a few weeks he had practically become a marksman.

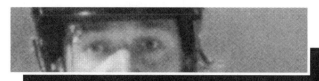

Marksmanship was not the only field in which Russell felt he had to exceed his co-star. Perhaps owing to the hatred between the Cort and Herod characters, Russell initiated a private rivalry between himself and Hackman. Russell began poking almost childish jibes at Hackman's permed hairstyle. But as Russell later explained, "I was playing Gene's adversary. A lot had to do with the relationship between the characters."

Russell enjoyed a better rapport with Leonardo DiCaprio, just starting to come into his own both as an actor and a screen personality of presence.

The Quick and the Dead is a western revenge saga, the twist being that the protagonist is a mysterious female gunfighter named Ellen who is seeking vengeance for the brutal murder of her father (Gary Sinise in an effective cameo) at the hands of the appropriately named Herod. Herod has made himself the boss of the town ironically named Redemption and rules with a sadistic hand. Ellen, or "The Lady," intends to even the score by killing Hcrod in the final stage of the "shoot-to-kill" tournament, where the last man standing will be awarded a prize of $123,000. In the town, she discovers Cort, a former outlaw who rode with Herod, but who has found peace through God. Herod now regards Cort as his enemy, keeping him bound in chains until he is forced to partake in the tournament. Also, Herod's cocky son Fee, known as "The Kid," fancies himself as fast a draw as his father. In the tournament, Herod easily disposes of the competition, including Ace Hanlon and even his own son. He apparently also takes down Ellen, but it is all a setup devised by the woman and Cort, who kill Herod in the final shootout.

Interestingly, *The Quick and the Dead* was never intended as serious western drama, but rather a parody of the genre, particularly the Italian westerns that had made a star out of Clint Eastwood during the 1960s. Gene Hackman plays his role broadly, but Stone, DiCaprio and Crowe execute their parts with an earnestness that gives the film a solemnity not intended by director Raimi.

This mixed message was pointed out by critical reviews of the movie. *The Quick and the Dead* was released in February 1995 and was immediately trashed by the critics. Steven Rea of the *Philadelphia Inquirer* perhaps offered the most scathing attack against the film by calling it "a kind of *Mad* magazine version of a spaghetti western, a lost Sergio Leone epic with impudent, cartoonish sensibility."

Leonard Maltin's *Movie Guide* called the film "a sluggish western (that) tries to turn Sharon Stone into The Man With No Name, but even on a parody level, it doesn't work."

Sharon Stone was upset at the critical panning her film received. She had hoped that *The Quick and the Dead* would establish her both as a serious actress and a force to be reckoned with in Hollywood.

In fairness however, there were a few critical accolades for the picture, including a review that called the film "both a homage to the spaghetti western and a clever send-up of the genre's best-known clichés."

It was Gene Hackman who walked away with the acting kudos, with Leonardo DiCaprio a close second. Russell was

The Quick and the Dead (1995)

hardly noted for his work, which proved extremely disappointing given the potential of the project.

Russell received few reviewer comments regarding his work in the picture. A *Washington Post* critic provided a back-handed compliment when he wrote that Russell Crowe's "pretty Australian face" would attract better film work in the future.

Actually, it was Sharon Stone who provided Russell with his best-publicized review when she remarked, "Russell Crowe is the sexiest actor working in movies today." Stone's comment both surprised and flattered the actor.

> As for Russell's feelings regarding the picture, he basically agreed with most critics and said that "The movie is riddled with clichés." Lamenting his own participation in such a project, he added, "I'm really looking forward to participating in movies that don't have either 'dark' or 'dead' in the title."

Despite his disappointment over the failure of *The Quick and the Dead*, Russell remained grateful to Sharon Stone for providing him with his first big Hollywood break. But now his determination to chart his own course led him in an interesting direction. He rejected offers to appear in major studio films to accept an assignment in a $1.3 million independent feature called *No Way Back*.

"They may have been more expensive projects," Russell noted. "But most of the 30-odd studio offers I received were variations of the same story."

In *No Way Back*, Russell plays FBI agent Zack Grant, whose partner is killed during an assignment that goes wrong. Mobster Frank Serlano, played by Michael Lerner, loses his son in the same operation and kidnaps Zack's son in retaliation. To get his son back, Zack must kill the Yakuza assassin, Yuji Kobayashi, portrayed by Asian actor Etsushi Toyokawa, who is responsible for the death of the mobster's son. The part provided Russell with a character who was a complete role reversal from the despicable Hando in *Romper Stomper*. The film also features Canadian actress Helen Slater, cast as the chatty airline stewardess, Mary, who attempts to assist Russell in his investigation.

The film offered Russell the opportunity to play a father for the first time onscreen, and he hoped his role might put to rest all the bad publicity he was still receiving from *Romper Stomper*. But *No Way Back* is not a movie of which Russell feels particularly proud. The only satisfaction he derived from the picture was his association with Helen Slater, whom he appreciated because of her talents as a songwriter.

No Way Back had its first showing in Japan in 1995, but was never released theatrically in North America. Columbia Tri-Star felt the picture wasn't strong enough to attract Western audiences and instead decided to premiere the movie on HBO before releasing it on videocassette, where it made little impact.

No Way Back (1995)

Apparently, Russell's personal life wasn't faring much better. He and Danielle were experiencing difficulties based on her decision to focus on her own career and not live in the shadow of Russell's potential success. These difficulties were further exacerbated by Russell's lengthy location shoots, which he tried to make up for by frequent plaintive long-distance calls. She wasn't fond of the fast-paced Hollywood lifestyle that the publicity machine suggested Russell had begun to embrace.

"Things were starting to happen for him," Danielle said to *New Idea* magazine, "and I didn't want to be in L.A."

Russell's view of their breakup was more of a shoulder shrug. "Even the Germans know how to have a good time, tell a few stories and have a few drinks."

In truth, Russell had desperately wanted to marry Danielle. But that was not going to happen. Both were single-minded in their ambitions—and neither was apparently willing to compromise.

No Way Back (1995)

On a positive note, Russell's film career continued to flourish. Even though *The Quick and the Dead* failed to create a commercial splash at the box office, Russell continued to receive a number of script offers, including a science-fiction movie called *Virtuosity*. He accepted a role in the cyber-thriller, budgeted at $14 million, which dealt with a computer-generated serial killer intended to assist police trainees in simulated crime investigations. Problems arise when the killer is fed too much intelligence and eventually escapes into the real world. Russell plays SID 6.7 (an acronym for "Sadistic, Intelligent and Dangerous"), the robot that creates chaos for Lieutenant Parker Barnes, played by Denzel Washington, and Dr. Madison Carter, portrayed by Kelly Lynch, as it went on a spree of mayhem and murder.

Director Brett Leonard was not unfamiliar with the technological aspects of the film, having directed *The Lawnmower Man* in 1992 that was loosely based on the Stephen King short story of the same name. The special effects he employed at the time were impressive technological inroads, but by the time *Virtuosity* was made three years later, CGI (computer-generated imagery) had advanced to a whole new level.

Fighting to get the role of SID 6.7, Russell must have experienced a sense of *déjà vu*. As with *The Quick and the Dead*, the producing studio did not want to use him. Paramount Pictures invested a lot of money in the project, and Russell did not seem a bankable prospect, especially paired against A-list actor Denzel Washington.

Fortunately, director Leonard, who had been soliciting Russell for the movie through direct correspondence, held fast to his

Virtuosity (1995)

choice, and though it took Paramount seven months to acquiesce, the studio agreed to give Russell a screen test. The actor may have bristled both personally and professionally at having to audition for the part after he had established himself in other roles, but he accepted—in his test he spit directly into megastar Denzel Washington's face.

According to Russell, the expectoration was accidental. "It was a scene where I'm in a wire cage, and Denzel is on the other side. I decided to pump it up a bit, and once the director calls 'Action!' I jump down off this thing and start screaming at Denzel. The scene was very dialogue heavy for me. But with the very first word I say, spittle comes flying out of my mouth and lands right onto Denzel's lips."

Russell would always credit his co-star for his professionalism. "You know, most actors would have been out of there. But Denzel knew it was my screen test, and he knows that if either he moves or if my mind moves into the reality of what has just happened, he'll screw up my concentration. So he carries on with the scene."

After the test, however, Denzel began mock screaming at Russell before breaking into laughter.

Russell won the role, but as he later reported, "Only because Denzel wanted me."

The role of SID 6.7 was not unlike the violent Hando from *Romper Stomper*. However, the film relicd heavily on technical gimmickry, including computer-generated effects, meaning that Russell performed mostly in front of a blue screen, and the scenery and such were superimposed later. This technique can prove difficult unless the actor is gifted with imagination and fully understands the story.

Fortunately, Russell scored on both points and was pleased when he saw the results. His interaction with imaginary props was totally believable in the finished film. Russell delivered a frighteningly believable portrayal of a robot programmed with the evil and cunning intelligence of the most notorious killers of history, including Adolph Hitler, Charles Manson and Ted Bundy.

> **Director Brett Leonard was so impressed with Russell that he hailed him as the new James Cagney. Despite the Aussie's reputation for arrogance, Leonard also said that working with Crowe was the best part of making the film.**

Despite the intriguing subject matter and top-notch performances from all of the cast that included William Forsythe, Louise Fletcher and Costas Mandylor, *Virtuosity* was not an overwhelming critical or commercial success when it was released in 1995. The picture grossed $24,048,000, which placed it just slightly higher than *The Quick and the Dead*'s $18,636,000.

Several critics did, however, favorably note Russell's performance. Jay Carr from the *Boston Globe* wrote: " [*Virtuosity*] largely wastes the wit and mischief in Australian actor Russell Crowe's performance."

Russell delivered a frighteningly believable portrayal of a robot programmed with the evil and cunning intelligence of the most notorious killers of history, including Adolph Hitler, Charles Manson and Ted Bundy.

Virtuosity (1995)

Russell later contrasted American and Australian filmmaking by saying that North American productions had a tendency to focus more on technical and special effects elements whereas in Australia "we tell stories."

> **He was pleased, however, with director Leonard's decision to close the film with the song _The Photograph Kills_, a number recorded by Russell's band, 30 Odd Foot Of Grunts.**

Russell suddenly found himself a hot property in Hollywood, and he was inundated with scripts. He chose to appear opposite Bridget Fonda in a strange "little" movie called _Rough Magic_. Based on the novel _Miss Shumway Waves a Wand_ by James Hadley Chase, the film is set in 1949 and tells of Myra (Fonda), a magician's assistant, who flees to Mexico after she witnesses her boyfriend Cliff (D.W. Moffett) murder her boss. Russell plays Alec Ross, who is hired by the boyfriend to locate and keep tabs on Myra until Cliff arrives. Naturally the two fall in love, and the film takes a silly turn as the couple embarks on a search for a "magic elixir."

Apparently, it was Bridget Fonda who requested Russell for the role of Alec Ross. And Russell was eager to play a romantic part with Fonda, who had enjoyed such screen successes as _Single White Female_ and _Singles_. She had also recently been named as one of the 100 sexiest stars in film, which certainly proved another attraction for Russell.

Russell suddenly found himself a hot property in Hollywood, and he was inundated with scripts.

Despite his enjoyment of working both with Fonda and French director Clare Peploe, Russell failed to score a success with _Rough Magic_. Part of the problem was Peploe's decision to remove many of the comedic elements from Chase's novel so that the final

CROWE FAN FACT

Russell's acting talent, versatility and temperament have resulted in his being heralded as the new Clark Gable, the new James Dean, the new Robert Mitchum, the new Marlon Brando, the new Mickey Rourke and the new Nick Nolte.

film uncomfortably mixes two distinctly different genres—film noir (with a particular nod to the Robert Mitchum/Jane Greer classic *Out of the Past*) and magic realism—in a flat, basically humorless format.

Critics naturally were brutal to the May 1997 release. *San Francisco Examiner* critic Barbara Shulgasser's comments were representative of the negative feedback. She wrote in a scathing review called "*Magic* Is Rough on the Audience," "Just as Fonda is technically beautiful, but generally a lifeless actress, Peploe is technically proficient but generally misses every opportunity for believable human interaction and the humor that often results."

Russell, perhaps fortunately, received little mention in most of the reviews, although Roger Ebert called him "steady" in "the Mitchum role." Perhaps the most perceptive comment came from John Anderson, who mentioned in his *Los Angeles Times* review that Russell Crowe is "talented but consistently misused"—an accurate assessment regarding Russell's onscreen capabilities. But that was about to change.

chapter 6

Crowe Confidential

These were difficult days for Russell Crowe.

He was still hurting from his breakup with Danielle Spencer. Though both had offered colorful comments to the press regarding their split, the bottom line was that they still cared deeply for one another. Russell, in fact, said that since he turned 30, he was giving more thought to having children, adding with a typical Crowe quip, "Shocking, huh? I never thought I'd be speaking like this."

Regarding a potential commitment to Danielle, Russell said, "I have a few work obligations I need to fulfill. Then I want to focus on the woman I love and see if I can't create something more permanent."

Danielle was sympathetic to Russell's public press, but perhaps suspicious of his often-flowery sincerity. She could see that Russell's main focus was still on his work.

The movie *L.A. Confidential* is based on the novel by crime writer James Ellroy, who took his *Confidential* title from a popular entertainment sleaze magazine predominant in the 1950s. Its scandal sheet format was the forerunner of today's supermarket "rag" publications. Russell immediately wanted a role in the film, but he doubted that his credentials were strong enough.

Director Curtis Hanson thought differently. He really didn't want superstars in the film. In fact, the city itself would be the main character. But he needed a strong cast to support the backdrop of vintage Los Angeles.

> Though both had offered colorful comments to the press regarding their split, the bottom line was that they still cared deeply for one another.

L.A. Confidential (1997)

During the 1950s, L.A. had already become a noir-ish metropolis far removed from the 1930s glamour of MGM and Clark Gable. The movies depicting Los Angeles had veered into a stark new realism, perhaps best exemplified by Anthony Mann's excursion into the depths of the city's criminal undercurrent, *He Walked by Night*, which was produced in 1948.

Another film representative of the era (if not the place) was the 1950 picture *The Asphalt Jungle*, featuring a superlative ensemble cast not of top-line actors, but made up of strong characters such as Sterling Hayden, Louis Calhern, James Whitmore, Marc Lawrence and, in a lesser role, Marilyn Monroe. The picture de-glamorizes and ultimately punishes its criminal perpetrators while leaving the city itself with a questionable bill of health. This was paralleled in the central theme of *L.A. Confidential*, with added doses of perverted ambition and police corruption (touched upon to a lesser degree in the 1950 John Huston film).

Hanson already had Russell in mind for the part of Officer Wendell "Bud" White, one of a trio of L.A. detectives involved in scandal and corruption centered around the Los Angeles Police Department during the 1950s.

Hanson told Russell during casting that the character of Bud White possessed the same force and inner rage that Crowe had employed to such startling effect as Hando in *Romper Stomper*. White was a man who worked within the constraints of the law—but just barely. And when dealing with particularly sleazy or repellant characters, he also had no compunction about crossing even that barrier.

Russell was the first actor cast in this picture that proved to be an ensemble piece à la *The Asphalt Jungle*. His fellow officers were played by Kevin Spacey as the opportunistic Sergeant Jack Vincennes and Guy Pearce as the self-righteous Detective Lieutenant Ed Exley. The rest of the cast was rounded out by James

Cromwell as the crooked Captain Dudley Liam Smith, Danny DeVito as the sleazy scandal sheet editor Sid Hudgens and Kim Basinger who won the Best Supporting Actress Oscar for her role as the down-on-her-luck hooker Lynn Bracken (essaying the Marilyn Monroe part—or, more precisely, showcasing long-forgotten 1940s movie icon Veronica Lake).

L.A. Confidential tells the complicated, interweaving stories of three cops pursuing a murder investigation, each handling the case with his own agenda. During the course of the film, Kevin Spacey's character is suddenly murdered in a cold-blooded maneuver by the corrupt Captain Smith.

Russell's character undergoes his own assault at the picture's climax, but manages to survive, though it is not made clear whether he has regained all of his faculties after the gunfight as he tenders a slight wave to former rival/partner Ed Exley as he

L.A. Confidential (1997)

drives off with Kim Basinger. Nor is it shown that corruption no longer exists within the L.A. Detective Unit. The movie ends on an effective ambiguous note.

Critics praised the film, with Roger Ebert giving it a four-star review and calling it one of the best movies of the year. Richard Schickel of *Time* magazine concurred: "If you have to spend time in a labyrinth, these are the kind of guys to do it with."

> *L.A. Confidential* provided Russell with his biggest commercial success yet, earning $65 million, compared to the much-smaller $250,000 take from *Rough Magic*.

Russell was gratified to finally enjoy his first bona fide box office hit. Rather than capitalizing on his success and accepting the succession of tough-guy parts then on offer, he surprised the money-driven industry by returning to Australia to fulfill a commitment to appear in another small-budget (about $2.3 million), eclectic offering called *Heaven's Burning*.

Heaven's Burning thematically resembles *Romper Stomper* in that it deals with racism against the Asian community in Australia. The story was based on a true incident in which a Japanese woman faked her own kidnapping while on her honeymoon in Sydney to escape an unhappy marriage that, per custom, had been arranged by her parents.

In the film, the character of Midori (Youki Kudoh) likewise devises her own kidnapping for the same reason, only to become involved in a series of misadventures alongside the

Rather than capitalizing on his success and accepting the succession of tough-guy parts then on offer, he surprised the money-driven industry by returning to Australia...

Russell Crowe character, Colin O'Brien, a garage owner/getaway driver for Afghan gang members.

Russell sported a unique "Elvis-like" look for the movie, including slicked-back hair and prominent sideburns, and he played the role with a tough machismo. He still hadn't completely shed his *L.A. Confidential* character. Elements of Bud White came through both on- and offscreen, with Russell often presenting a moody or confrontational personality on set.

Still, director Craig Lahiff spoke in the highest terms of Russell's professionalism before the camera: "He's extremely intense when he's working. He's always trying to give more than 100 percent in his performance."

Heaven's Burning (1997)

Unfortunately, *Heaven's Burning* never caught on with the movie-going public either in its home country or in the North American market when it was released in 1997, and it has since virtually disappeared from public view. Critics likewise regarded the film with little admiration, with one referring to *Heaven's Burning* as "*Reservoir Dingoes.*"

> Russell's career remained on a roll, however. He had his pick of projects, and his choices were often eclectic. His next picture, **Breaking Up**, is a good example of his eccentricity in choosing film roles that are not necessarily beneficial to achieving stardom.

The movie was written by Pulitzer Prize-winning playwright Michael Cristofer and directed by Robert Greenwald, whose previous efforts included the critically acclaimed television drama *The Burning Bed*, which successfully transformed Farrah Fawcett from a TV sex kitten into a serious actress. Most of Greenwald's other films, though, were hardly up to that standard.

Breaking Up was destined to become a commercial failure, owing to the fact that it was a low budget, short (28-day) production shoot that consisted basically of relationship dialogue between two people: Steve (Crowe) and Monica (Salma Hayek). Perhaps Russell accepted this project because it challenged his acting capabilities. With such a short shooting schedule and so much dialogue to learn, the actor had to learn his lines and develop his character quickly. In addition, he faced the responsibility of conveying believability in a story that cast its theme of the love affair

> Perhaps Russell accepted this project because it challenged his acting capabilities.

Breaking Up (1997)

between an Australian man and a Mexican woman against the backdrop of New York City.

Russell lived up to the task of creating a full-blooded character, but his preparation and hard work did little to entice the public to embrace the film. The movie was released to only *three* theaters! The critics were a little more generous, with Ian Hodder from *Boxoffice* writing, "*Breaking Up* is a good movie, but it doesn't have enough zingy lines or story innovations to rise above the level of protypical romantic comedy."

> **The compliments of Russell's co-star carried the most weight. According to Salma Hayek, "Russell was the best actor I'd ever worked with."**

The truth was that while he was in demand, *L.A. Confidential* was Russell's only true hit. Of course, his lack of box office success was his own choice, with Russell forsaking highly publicized studio pictures in favour of small independent productions that offered little chance of being seen by the general public. The larger-budget films such as *The Quick and the Dead* and *Virtuosity* that he had appeared in unfortunately had also failed to generate much excitement at the box office, but the fact was that Russell was not intent on achieving "stardom." It was the craft of acting, the challenge of experimenting with a character that motivated him. He wanted to be recognized in Hollywood, but as a serious and versatile actor. He did not want to sacrifice his artistic integrity to the temptation of quick riches and tabloid fame.

He wanted to be recognized in Hollywood, but as a serious and versatile actor.

Russell was offered the opportunity to sign a four-picture deal with

Miramax Films, but he resisted because he didn't want to lose the independence to choose his own roles. Miramax, though, was so eager to sign Russell that studio head Harvey Weinstein submitted seven of the studio's top scripts—all but one of which were rejected by the actor.

The property that Russell found most appealing was a period romantic comedy called _Shakespeare in Love_. Unfortunately, the meeting arranged by Miramax between Russell and British director John Madden proved a disaster when Madden frankly told the actor that he did not think Russell was right for the part. Russell responded by telling Madden to "Go f*** yourself."

However, Russell had better luck in his meetings with the director of his next project. David E. Kelley was best known for his television work on such shows as _Ally McBeal_ and _The Practice_. Together with writer Sean O'Byrne, Kelley prepared a screenplay for a movie called _Mystery, Alaska_, to be directed by Jay Roach for Disney. Russell was offered the part of Sheriff John Biebe, the star player of Mystery, Alaska's (population: 633) amateur hockey team. Outside of hockey, nothing much happens in the town, and that sport is Mystery's main interest. Events escalate when the town team is invited to play against the New York Rangers in a televised game. Although planned as a publicity stunt, the "Mystery Boys" prove their mettle in the climactic game.

Russell faced a new challenge to prepare for the role: he had to learn how to ice skate, just as he'd had to learn to handle a gun with proficiency for _The Quick and the Dead_. He underwent a rigorous six-week training program to learn to maneuver convincingly on the ice. To prepare himself psychologically for the competitive edge needed for his character, each day Russell ran up a flag of the Southern Cross—identifying both Australia and New Zealand—and then had the cast sing their respective national anthems before hitting the ice.

Filming for the picture took place in Canmore, Alberta, in early January 1998. Co-starring with Russell was Burt Reynolds, who had slipped into successful character roles after enjoying many years as the top box office draw in the world in the late 1970s. Reynolds played Judge Walter Burns, a former hockey sensation whose son is a member of the team.

The film proved an uncomfortable production given the often −5° to −20° F temperatures prevalent during Canadian winters. While Russell enjoyed making the movie, once shooting wrapped, he was not unhappy to leave the frigid location.

Perhaps another reason for his eagerness to leave Alberta was that one night during the shooting of the picture, Russell and several members of the *Mystery, Alaska* crew got into a messy confrontation in a local pub with approximately 30 members of a timber crew. Apparently, Russell and his cronies had been drinking quite heavily, and offense was taken after Russell loudly exclaimed that "hockey was a game for wimps" and that Alberta was "boring." A huge fight ensued, with tables overturned, and chairs and everything else hurled in the melee.

Burt Reynolds later offered his own insight into the character of Russell Crowe: "There's a fire in him that

"There's a fire in him that burns all night long, all day long, all the time. And that may hurt him because people don't understand that kind of flame."

Mystery, Alaska (1999)

burns all night long, all day long, all the time. And that may hurt him because people don't understand that kind of flame."

Perhaps Russell has a temper; perhaps he can be outspoken and confrontational. But he is also a very fair man, and when executives at Disney suggested that *Mystery, Alaska* should be promoted as a Russell Crowe film, the actor immediately rejected the idea, stating that the picture was an ensemble piece and that one actor should not dominate it. He pointed out that, as in *L.A. Confidential*, the star of the film was the location: the fictional community of *Mystery, Alaska*.

Mystery, Alaska was another "small" film that did little at the box office when it was released in October 1999. The $28 million production earned back only $9 million in the United States.

Mystery, Alaska (1999)

CROWE FAN FACT

Producer Howard Baldwin, a former owner of the Pittsburgh Penguins hockey team, along with team members, helped teach Russell to skate. Weak ankles made it difficult for the actor to skate convincingly.

Critically, Russell fared much better. Despite competent playing by Reynolds and co-stars Hank Azaria, Mary McCormack and Maury Chaykin, it was Russell Crowe who scored acting honors. *Los Angeles Times* critic Kenneth Turan wrote: "It is Australian Russell Crowe . . . who gives the film's standout performance." Leonard Maltin's annual *Movie & Video Guide* gives the film two stars, but concludes its review: "Russell Crowe is the only one to rise above the material."

maximum
Crowe

The *Insider* is based on the true story of how tobacco company scientist Dr. Jeffrey Wigand was persuaded to expose damning information about the cigarette industry and how the investigative television program *60 Minutes* backed away from broadcasting the interview at first for fear of a multimillion-dollar lawsuit from tobacco companies. Wigand then went through a period where he was threatened and intimidated, eventually losing his home and his family.

Directed by Michael Mann, *The Insider* is a tragic film, but a captivating one. One of its many strengths is in its casting. Mann headed his cast with Al Pacino, whom he had earlier directed in the 1995 crime thriller *Heat*. Pacino plays the part of Lowell Bergman, the producer of *60 Minutes*, who persuades Wigand to "spill the beans" on national television. Canadian-born Christopher Plummer was chosen for the role of television journalist Mike Wallace and Broadway actress Diane Venora was picked for the part of Wigland's wife, Liane.

At first Russell was puzzled why he was offered the role of Wigand, who was much older and many pounds heavier. But when actor and director met to discuss the picture, Mann offered a simple explanation: "I'm not talking to you because of your weight or your age. I'm talking to you because of what you have inside." Mann was familiar with Russell's film work and had been particularly impressed with his role as Hando in *Romper Stomper*.

Russell responded to the director's faith in him by committing himself 100 percent to the role. He embarked on an intense six-week preparation

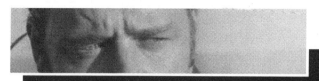

schedule that included spending many hours watching tapes of Wigand's testimony to allow him to perfect his portrayal of the man's mannerisms and American speech patterns. Then he went on a cheeseburger and bourbon binge, *sans* exercise, that saw him gain 48 pounds. To complete the physical transformation, he trimmed his hair to accommodate the wig he was required to wear. Finally, he changed his own natural manner of walking and adopted Wigand's unique short-step waddle.

Michael Mann thought it unnecessary for Russell to take on the physical demands of the role such as Robert De Niro had done in his impersonation of Jake LaMotta in *Raging Bull*, believing that the soul of the character was the most important element. But Russell disagreed: "Once I began researching the character, I realized that the physical transformation was necessary. Just as you can't effectively portray Abraham Lincoln with just a mustache. I had to understand how Jeffrey Wigand felt physically before I could deal with what was going on inside him."

What Russell adamantly did not want was a face-to-face meeting with the man he was about to play. He felt it was unnecessary, plus he didn't want to be told how he should do the part. However, just before the cameras were set to roll, Russell relented and agreed to shoot a few golf balls with Jeffrey Wigand. The actor later admitted that their meeting was beneficial.

"I felt we had to honor this man," Russell said. "He put everything on the line to tell the truth."

Russell was excited when filming began because, for the first time, he was playing a real person, which challenged him as an actor. He was also eager, and a little nervous, to work alongside Pacino (with whom he would be sharing most of his scenes) and the distinguished Christopher Plummer.

But the physical and emotional demands of the part came with a cost, and frequently he was exhausted by day's end. His social life became virtually nonexistent during the shoot as he'd usually fall into bed at night.

His temperament was also noticeably different on the set. Where Russell had previously been known to be argumentative and confrontational with his co-players, on *The Insider* his demeanor was pleasant and friendly.

He got along particularly well with eight-time Oscar nominee Al Pacino, though the two had totally opposite approaches to their acting. Russell is more methodical in his preparation, while Pacino prefers to work more spontaneously and act his scenes in the moment. But the two actors bonded personally over their shared love of baseball. Russell presented Pacino with a customized Louisville Slugger bat, and Pacino reciprocated the gesture by delivering Russell seven large cartons that contained the components of a baseball-pitching machine.

Russell also got along well with Michael Mann, although the actor did lose his temper with the director early in the production. Russell's first scene required him to merely walk through a doorway. Mann shot the scene 17 times

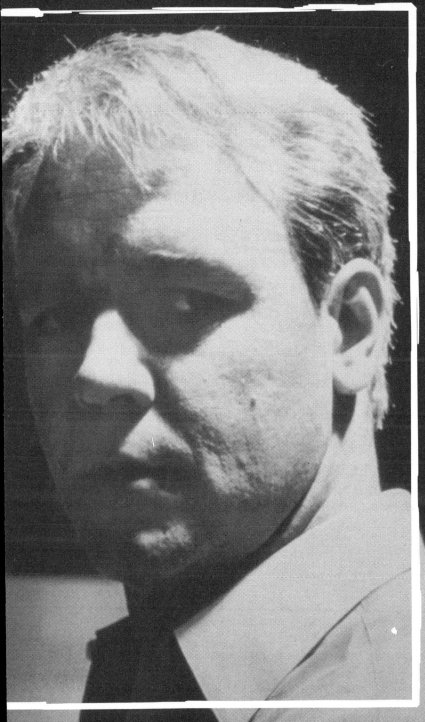

The Insider (1999)

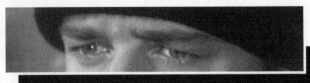

CROWE FAN FACT

During the filming of *The Insider*, the make-up department had so much trouble with Russell's long hair that he had to shave his head and wear a wig.

over a two-day period, apparently because he wasn't happy with the placement of a shadow on the wall. Finally, Russell exploded. Mann let him vent, and once the air had been cleared, the two worked respectfully with one another.

Russell was pleased with his work on *The Insider*, but he was also happy when the picture wrapped. He set about regaining his appearance, growing his hair back and losing the extra poundage that he had retained for five months. As with most overweight people, he found that adding the weight was much easier than dropping it. It took him another five months of diet and vigorous exercise before he was back to his normal weight. He was horrified to discover that as a result of his weight gain, his cholesterol level was dangerously high. In spite of this health concern and the picture's "dangers of smoking" message, Russell who had been smoking (and inhaling) since he was 10 continued his habit.

"I know it's terrible," he remarked. "But I'm a great fan of irony."

In the finished film, which was released in North America in November 1999, Russell's performance has been described as "spellbinding." Critics were unanimous in their praise. Janet Maslin in *The New York Times* commented that Russell is "a subtle powerhouse in his wrenching evocation of Dr. Wigand," while *The Los Angeles Times'* Kenneth Turan wrote that Russell Crowe "joins an old-fashioned masculine presence with an unnerving ability to completely disappear inside a role."

The accolades most appreciated by Russell came from his top-billed co-star, Al Pacino, who remarked, "I thought what he did was just brilliant!" and his real-life counterpart Jeffrey Wigand, who said: "My hat's off to Russell. He's got it down. He even looks like me."

Russell's final lines regarding the role were a tribute to the true-life character he played: "I think Jeffrey is a hero because he didn't go and pick up a gun."

For his work on the film, Russell earned a Golden Globe nomination (where he appeared accompanied by Jodie Foster) and his first Best Actor Oscar nomination (which he lost to his *L.A. Confidential* co-star Kevin Spacey, who won for his role in

The Insider (1999)

American Beauty). Russell was comically philosophical about his loss, saying, "I'm an Academy-nominated actor for the rest of my life, no matter what crap I do from here on in."

Russell took a well-deserved break after the rigors of filming *The Insider*, returning to Australia to relax on his ranch and jam with his band. He launched a new album called *Gaslight*, which contained 11 songs and was sold via the Internet and by mail order to ensure that the band's staunchest fans and early supporters were able to obtain a copy without difficulty.

> **Russell had finally received recognition as an international movie star, but he was not enjoying his growing celebrity. He played with his band at local hotel pubs and was accessible to the media, granting interviews to the Australian press.**

In answer to a reporter's question as to whether he was as dedicated to his music as to his acting, he replied, "I take my music seriously. It's another creative expression."

It was while Russell was still bloated and physically exhausted from playing Jeffrey Wigand that he was approached by his agent George Freeman about playing the part of the lean and muscular hero for a picture to be called *Gladiator*—a role apparently rejected by Tom Cruise. It was not exactly an enticing proposition to the overweight actor who could barely walk up a flight of steps without becoming winded. He also doubted the commercial value of such a project, since outside some Italian "epics," there hadn't been a gladiator picture made since *Spartacus*.

In answer to a reporter's question as to whether he was as dedicated to his music as to his acting, he replied, "I take my music seriously. It's another creative expression."

Russell's initial reaction was to say, "As if I am ever going to be in a gladiator film!"

Still, Russell was persuaded by Michael Mann to talk to the film's producer at DreamWorks to discuss the project.

It didn't take studio production head Walter Parkes long to convince him. Parkes, a formidable power since he ran DreamWorks in partnership with Steven Spielberg, merely said three things: "The story takes place in 185 AD; the director is Ridley Scott; and you start the film as a Roman general." Parkes had a most impressive track record, including the movies *The Mark of Zorro* and *Saving Private Ryan*.

> **What really piqued Russell's interest in the project was not the $100 million allocated to the production budget, but rather the opportunity to work with Ridley Scott, who had to his credit such successful and visually exciting films as *Alien* and *Blade Runner*. When the actor later met with Scott to discuss the film, the director outlined the project in detail, and the two sealed Russell's commitment with a handshake.**

Scott had his leading man, but he was determined to cast the other principal roles with recognizable faces who could likewise "deliver the goods." For the evil Emperor Commodus, he chose Joaquin Phoenix (brother of the late River). Connie Nielsen would play Commodus' sister, Lucilla. For added authenticity, Scott hired two veterans of period piece adventures, Richard Harris and Oliver Reed, to essay the roles of Emperor Marcus Aurelius and Antonius Proximo, respectively.

Although *Gladiator* would have an impressive supporting cast, it would be Russell Crowe as General Maximus Decimus Meridius who would carry the picture.

CROWE FAN FACT

Russell's character was originally called Narcissus Maximus, which didn't seem a strong enough name for a man who sets out on a journey to avenge the deaths of his wife and son. Russell made up the name Maximus Decimus Meridius, which he felt was better suited to a soldier and "flowed off the tongue."

That is, Russell and the movie's convincing computer-generated special effects. Convincing was the key word, because if any of the effects were flawed, the action sequences would lose their believability. Fortunately, Ridley Scott was one of the most technically proficient directors in the industry and painstakingly worked out each photographic "trick shot" with his team of technicians.

By the time shooting was slated to begin, Russell was back in shape and well rested from his Australian trip. He had even worked out to gain muscle for the physically demanding role.

The only problem Russell had with the part was deciphering the character's inner psychology. The closest he had come to a period piece was when he played the gunfighter-turned-preacher Cort in *The Quick and the Dead*. His other roles had been either contemporary or futuristic (*Virtuosity*). In *Gladiator*, he played what could be perceived as a second-century AD superhero, a character who on the surface was not apparently imbued with much psychological depth

Russell immersed himself in research, reading scores of books about the Roman Empire and marking specific passages that provided insight into the character. Finally, he discovered his inspiration in a book titled *Meditations*, written by Marcus

Gladiator (2000)

Aurelius. The passage that most intrigued him ends, *"And there is no man who is able to prevent this."*

To prepare for his role as a military general, Russell pulled together a group of his buddies and led them through a difficult bike trip through the Australian Outback. He furthered his preparation as an arena warrior by practicing for hours at a time, learning to master a sword for the intricate combat sequences. Then he underwent hours of training with former bodybuilding champion Ralf Moeller, who also plays a gladiator in the movie, to perfect the hand-to-hand combat scenes.

"This was not the first time I've had to act in a physically demanding part in a motion picture," Russell reported to the press. "But I have never had a role like this. I think in my next movie I'd like to play a bus driver."

> ***Gladiator*** is the story of Maximus Decimus Meridius, a Roman general who, following his army's defeat of Germanian tribes, returns in victory, hoping to soon be reunited with his family in Spain. However, instead of granting Maximus his simple request, Emperor Marcus Aurelius (Richard Harris) wishes for him to become the successor to his throne.

Political intrigue ensues when the emperor's son Commodus (Joaquin Phoenix) murders his father, succeeding him as emperor, then perceives Maximus as a threat. He orders the murder of Maximus along with his wife and son. Maximus escapes execution and flees to Spain to find his family has been killed. Eventually, Maximus is captured and sold as a gladiator, where he is trained in the art of gladiatorial combat by Antonius Proximo (Oliver Reed). Maximus proves himself an adept competitor in the arena, and he eventually returns to Rome where he battles to the death with Commodus before a cheering crowd.

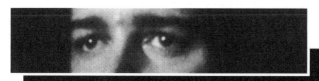

CROWE FAN FACT

When *Gladiator* began shooting, the script had not yet been completed. The scene in which Maximus (Crowe) talks about his home was ad-libbed— Russell described his own home in Australia, in particular the arrangement of the kitchen and the smells in the morning and at night.

Gladiator proved an incredibly difficult production. Despite Scott's tactical and technical preparation, neither he nor Russell was impressed with the special effects for the fight sequences. Because of these problems, battle scenes took much longer to film than had originally been anticipated.

The filming proved exceptionally grueling for Russell. All-day location shoots in England, Morocco and Malta had Russell enacting vigorous action sequences under the mercilessly hot sun while fitted in heavy armor and wielding a weighty sword.

To adhere to the rigid (and costly) shooting schedule, the actors were given only one day off per week to recharge their batteries. Russell chose to unwind by playing soccer. When the production company learned of his spare time activity, they requested that he not take part in *any* activity in which he might be injured.

Russell wrote back: "Dear Studio, I can wrestle with four tigers, but I can't play a game of soccer? Get over it. Love, Russell"

During the film, he certainly ran some serious risks. Live animals were used in the making of the movie to make the arena scenes appear as realistic as possible. While elephants, giraffes, leopards and zebras were shown to maximum effect, it was the tigers who really were the stars of the picture. Battling and defeating the predatory cats is Maximus's last challenge before facing Commodus in the arena.

Gladiator (2000)

Of course, working with such unpredictable beasts was hazardous. Russell refused to use a stand-in, but perhaps he thought of reconsidering when one of the handlers was almost fatally mauled after one of the tigers knocked him to the ground. Still, despite the seriousness of the mishap, Russell was determined to act his own scenes—within reason—to add authenticity to the filming.

"It was really a kind of a visceral experience," he explained. "It was full on. The tiger sequence is very complicated, and naturally I did not do everything in the sequence. But I got to do a couple of things where I hit the deck and the tiger comes at me. When you roll out of the way of the tiger and 1800 people go 'Ooooohhhh' immediately, it's kind of cool."

During production, Russell sustained his share of injuries, including a broken leg bone and a fractured hipbone. On different occasions he wrenched both biceps tendons out of their sockets (but he popped them back into place himself).

The worst tragedy to occur during filming was the sudden death of Oliver Reed, who collapsed while drinking in a pub in Malta in May 1999. The 61-year-old actor was better known in some circles for his carousing than for his acting talent. His death came as a hard blow to the cast and crew. He hadn't yet completed all of his scenes and director Scott was required to use a body double and computer imagery to fill in for the actor, which added $3 million to production costs. He was also forced to revise the script, which originally saw Antonius Proximo survive to the film's end credits.

Russell frequently surrendered to the pressures of the production by engaging in heated exchanges with Scott. Scott responded to Russell with patience and

> Still, despite the seriousness of the mishap, Russell was determined to act his own scenes— within reason—to add authenticity to the filming.

maintained his control as director. One of Russell's complaints concerned Scott's decision to eliminate the love scenes between Maximus and his wife, played by actress Giannina Facio. Scott's decision may have been based on other than artistic reasons, as Facio was Ridley Scott's girlfriend and he may have feared a real-life romance developing between the two actors.

Despite the frequent friction between the star and the director, Scott admired and commented upon Russell's generosity in advising the younger actors how a scene might best be played.

"He was extremely helpful to Joaquin and Connie," Scott recalled.

Russell was flexible on many points, but he would not bend on DreamWork's insistence that the movie's story have a conclusion. As he later put it: "Maximus has to die. What's he going to do if he doesn't? Open a pizza parlor outside the Coliseum and sell autographs?"

Maximus does die, in an exciting finale in which he is stabbed by the villainous Commodus before being taken into the arena for a final showdown with the Emperor. Maximus manages to kill the emperor before dying himself.

What many filmgoers did not realize is that *Gladiator* is based in fact. A dictator named Commodus *did* exist, and his cruelties exceed those portrayed onscreen by Joaquin Phoenix. His excesses and debaucheries apparently surpassed those of the more notorious Caligula.

Russell's concern about the box office potency of *Gladiator* proved unfounded. The film was released in May 2000 and went on to gross $457 million worldwide.

Critics were not stinting in their praise either. Russell was lauded for his performance and was even named "Superstar of 2000" by the London *Daily Mail*. The *Philadelphia Inquirer* called the film a "stunning achievement," giving a special acknowledgment to Russell: "But its impact as a movie flows from Russell Crowe, who is that rarity: a great actor who is fully up to the demands of playing a man of action."

Leonard Maltin's *2005 Movie & Video Guide* reports that "Russell Crowe is so good in his performance that one is willing to forgive story lulls."

> Richard Corliss of *Time* magazine agreed, but added a personal bias in his review: "Crowe could be a nicer fellow but hardly a better actor."

One of the less enthusiastic reviews came from *Chicago Sun-Times* critic Roger Ebert, who gave the film only two stars. While he wrote that Russell was "efficient" in his role of Maximus, he felt that most of the other actors were inadequate.

Regardless, the film was an enormous hit. Even Russell (who generally disliked seeing himself onscreen) attended a showing with Michael Mann and became excited when he watched the action unfold. Apparently, he jumped to his feet and applauded his many athletic endeavors.

> He'd finally arrived at a level of recognition dreamed of by other actors, but he still maintained emotional equilibrium, perhaps because it had been an uphill battle and success achieved through dedication and hard work.

Russell Crowe had become a bona fide superstar. His name on its own on the marquee could sell tickets.

Russell was jaded at this point and refused to seriously acknowledge his Hollywood celebrity status. He'd finally arrived at a level of recognition dreamed of by other actors, but he still maintained emotional equilibrium, perhaps because it had been an uphill battle and success achieved through dedication and hard work. He did not capitulate to pandering and adulation, which he regarded as superfluous trappings to what mattered most to him—the content and challenge of his work.

Nowhere was his commitment to the craft more proven than in his next role in a motion picture, his most challenging to date, where he was again called upon to play a flesh-and-blood person.

But first there was another date at the Academy Awards.

chapter 8

Oscar comes to call

Russell had no illusions about how easy it would be to achieve the ultimate industry honor, the Academy Award. He did not hold his breath about the chances of victory of his nominated characterization of Maximus over his arena rivals. In 2001, his fellow Best Actor contenders were a formidable group. Two-time Best Actor winner Tom Hanks was up yet again for his work in *Cast Away*. Ed Harris had earned a well-deserved nomination for *Pollock*. Geoffrey Rush was another strong competitor for *Quills*, as was the Spanish actor Javier Bardem for *Before Night Falls*.

A more frivolous accolade was awarded Russell Crowe when his *Gladiator* impersonation of Maximus was voted the sexiest cinema character *ever* in a 2001 poll for *Empire* magazine. Although frivolous, the award had some merit, seeing that he beat out such contenders as Harrison Ford as Indiana Jones, who rated fourth, and even besting Paul Newman and Robert Redford for their roles as Butch Cassidy and the Sundance Kid, the various incarnations of James Bond (portrayed by Sean Connery, George Lazenby, Roger Moore, Timothy Dalton and Pierce Brosnan), Brad Pitt in *Thelma and Louise,* and Clark Gable as the immortal Rhett Butler in *Gone with the Wind.*

Initially, Russell seemed a long shot in the Oscar competitions, placed as he was against Tom Hanks who had already been awarded the Golden Globe for his work in *Cast Away*. Generally, the winner of

---

A more frivolous accolade was awarded Russell Crowe when his *Gladiator* impersonation of Maximus was voted the sexiest cinema character ever in a 2001 poll for *Empire* magazine.

CROWE FAN FACT

Russell was offered, but turned down, the role of Logan/Wolverine in the film *X-Men* (2000).

that award is considered the odds-on favorite to win Hollywood's most coveted prize.

However, *Gladiator* itself had stacked up an impressive 11 Oscar nominations. Within the motion picture industry, the movie's wave of nominations could increase Russell's chances of winning the award.

In the meantime, Russell engaged in a very public, private life, having been seen in the company of Courtney Love, widow of Nirvana singer Kurt Cobain, who perhaps had achieved more infamy for his shotgun suicide than his music. Russell had known Courtney for a while before the two became even better acquainted following the Golden Globe awards ceremonies.

Courtney, though, was dealing with her own problems. At a Hollywood party, she apparently lashed out at Russell that it was she and not he who was the true "star." She was clearly intoxicated and not the best PR for the Oscar contender. Later, when Russell fell into the arms of Danielle Spencer, whom he'd invited as his date to the Oscar ceremonies, Courtney went into a rage, swearing and screaming as their limousine drove off. Of course, this exhibition made headlines, but fortunately the Oscar ballots had already been cast so the public disgrace could not change the vote.

On a lighter note during this heady period, Russell was approached at a party by Robert De Niro, who merely nodded approvingly to Russell before walking away—a gesture indicative of De Niro's extremely reserved personality, but one much appreciated by Crowe.

Also, upon meeting Tom Hanks, Russell and his fellow Oscar contender made a bet that whomever was the loser come Oscar night would clean the other's bathroom. One wonders if Tom Hanks honored the bet.

On the night of March 25, Russell proudly squired Danielle to the Academy Awards ceremony, accompanied by his mother and father. Meg Ryan, with whom Russell had apparently initiated an affair, decided to stay at home and watch the awards on television. She did, however, gift Russell with a good luck charm—a silver cross that was inscribed with words lifted from Banjo Peterson's *Clancy of the Overflow: "And he sees the vision splendid of the sunlit plains extended and at night the wondrous glory of the everlasting stars."*

Hilary Swank had won the previous year's Best Actress Award for *Boys Don't Cry*, and per Academy custom, it was her duty to announce the following year's Best Actor nominees and make the presentation to the winner. Many thought that Tom Hanks would pull a record three-time coup as Best Actor, beating out Spencer Tracy's record of two wins in a row, in 1937–38 for *Captains Courageous* and *Boy's Town*.

But when Hilary opened the envelope, the name she called was…Russell Crowe for *Gladiator*!

Despite the criticism Russell had endured in his personal and professional life, he was modest and appreciative in his acceptance speech. He gave a very special acknowledgment to his grandfather Stan Wemyss. Russell wore the red ribbon and cross of the MBE (Member of the British Empire) as tributes to his grandfather, whom Russell had respected both as a man and as a mentor to his own career ambitions.

> Russell Crowe, who was initially reluctant to appear in *Gladiator*, was later thrilled with his participation in the picture.

Speaking before others in the film industry and a television audience numbering in the millions, Russell gave a special acknowledgment to his parents "Who I just don't thank enough."

Russell, after expressing his appreciation to his co-stars and the other production talent, noted in his acceptance all the other budding talents both in show business and those embarking in other endeavors of life: "When you're growing up in the suburbs of Sydney or Auckland or Newcastle, you know a dream like this seems vaguely ludicrous and completely unobtainable, but this moment is directly connected to those childhood imaginings. And for anybody who is on the downside of advantage and relying purely on courage, it is possible."

Russell's acceptance speech, eloquent, pure and simple, is acknowledged as a close second to Don Ameche's memorable moment at the Oscar ceremonies when he was awarded the Best Supporting Actor prize in 1985 for *Cocoon*.

Gladiator, a film that many, including Russell Crowe himself, thought outdated in subject matter and not an audience favorite, won Academy Awards for Best Visual Effects, Best Costume Design (naturally), Best Sound—and ultimately, Best Picture. Sadly, Ridley Scott was passed over as Best Director in favor of Steven Sonderbergh, who won for *Traffic*.

Russell Crowe, who was initially reluctant to appear in *Gladiator*, was later thrilled with his participation in the picture.

"I believe *Gladiator* is a great movie and deserves to be acknowledged," he said.

meeting
Meg

Russell Crowe had received the film industry's highest tribute. He was also honored and flattered by the compliments of fellow actors, particularly the legendary Charlton Heston, whose title role in the 1959 film *Ben-Hur* had perhaps paved the way for Russell's later success.

Heston said, "Russell richly deserved the Oscar. As he came running down to receive it, I said to him, 'As one gladiator to another, I applaud you.'"

Russell certainly enjoyed the applause and recognition of the evening, but once the celebrations were over, it was time to get back to work. There were pictures in the wings—along with a substantially increased paycheck.

Proof of Life was a movie not initially intended for Russell Crowe. The two actors first

considered for the project were Meg Ryan and Mel Gibson. Meg Ryan had scored big with producers ever since her role opposite Billy Crystal in the 1989 hit *When Harry Met Sally*. Although she was popular with movie audiences, she really hadn't expressed much range as an actress, virtually playing the same character in *Sleepless in Seattle* (1993) and in *You've Got Mail* (1998), both starring Tom Hanks. Arguably, her most challenging screen role had been in the 1996 movie *Courage Under Fire*.

Of course, Mel Gibson had become a phenomenal movie success with his roles in the *Lethal Weapon* series, along with strong excursions into more dramatic fare, even including an attempt into Shakespeare with *Hamlet*. Mel rejected the film, claiming that the part wasn't right for

CROWE FAN FACT

Russell speaks with an Australian accent in the film, the first time he does so in an American production.

him. But Meg agreed to appear in the movie, surely prompted by a $15 million salary.

Director Taylor Hackford, who had previously helmed the 1982 Richard Gere box office hit *An Officer and a Gentleman*, did not have to look far to secure his leading man. Russell Crowe was available and definitely affordable—far beneath Mel Gibson's asking price.

> Yet again, Hackford initially received casting objection from the studio. Russell had not yet been Academy-recognized either for ***The Insider*** or ***Gladiator*** and was still not considered potent box office.

One of Hackford's strengths as a director was his ability to draw screen chemistry between his leading players, such as the magnetism between Richard Gere and Debra Winger in *An Officer and a Gentleman*, Keanu Reeves and Charlize Theron in *The Devil's Advocate* and Jeff Bridges and Rachel Ward in *Against All Odds*. Hackford understood that *Proof of Life* was not a traditional love story and that much of its success would depend on the relationship between its leading co-players.

The director admired Russell's strength of character, which he perceived imperative to the role, but he also liked and wanted the Australian element, even more inherent in Russell than in

Mel Gibson, who was born in America. Hackford persisted and finally landed Russell for the role.

The picture had been afforded an expansive multimillion-dollar budget and was to be shot on location, mostly in Ecuador, during a four-month filming schedule.

Proof of Life is a movie that has its basis in reality, drawing primarily from a story that was published in *Vanity Fair* concerning a professional hostage negotiator. The film features Russell as Terry Thorne, a negotiator who agrees to help Alice Bowman (Meg Ryan) negotiate the release of her husband Peter (David Morse), an oil company engineer who has been kidnapped by South American rebels. But Terry becomes infatuated with Alice and agrees to perform the hostage negotiations for free. Alice must raise nearly $1 million in cash so that Terry can act as an intermediary and pay off the terrorists. Complications arise, negotiations collapse and Terry treks off into the jungle to personally rescue Peter.

"I was amazed at his toughness," said director Hackford. "It was a difficult shoot, but Russell went into it all the way. He's thorny. He challenges you right back—and keeps everything alive."

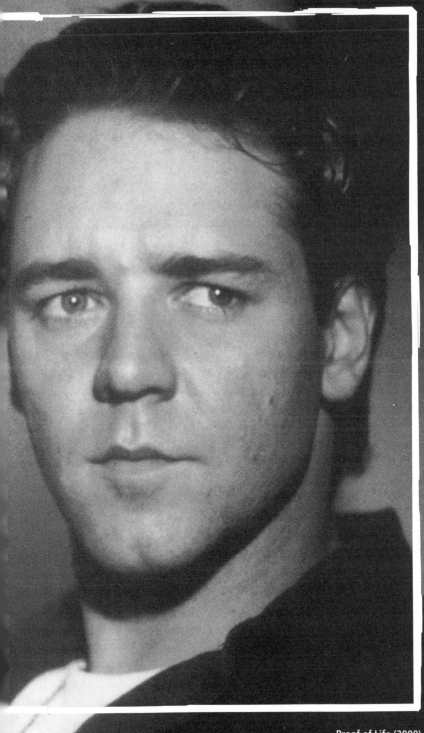

Proof of Life (2000)

Perhaps the production moved along smoothly, but suddenly there appeared a well-publicized conflict in one star player's personal life.

Russell was still single and free. However, Meg Ryan had been reported as enjoying a very stable and happy marriage to actor Dennis Quaid, perhaps best known at that point for his impersonation of Jerry Lee Lewis in the 1989 film *Great Balls of Fire*. Apparently an instant attraction developed between Russell and Meg on the set of *Proof of Life*. During the filming, the relationship between the two graduated into more than infatuation, and soon the tabloids were writing that Meg had left Dennis to begin an affair with Russell.

Proof of Life was released in December 2000. It proved a disappointing follow up to *Gladiator*, earning only $32,598,911 in domestic box office receipts. The movie would eventually make just over $50 million worldwide, but that was still far below its production cost. Most critics, as well, were harsh in their reviews of the picture. Sadly, it appeared that most of the negative reviews were based more on Russell and Meg Ryan's affair than on the quality of the movie itself.

For instance, *Time* magazine's Richard Corliss wrote, "The

Sadly, it appeared that most of the negative reviews were based more on Russell and Meg Ryan's affair than on the quality of the movie itself.

Proof of Life (2000)

all-American blonde is now a Jezebel, her cuddlings with Crowe sprayed across the covers of gossip magazines and on tabloid-tale TV shows. The eventual film looked destined to be remembered as Exhibit A in the trial of adulterous love."

Los Angeles Times critic Kenneth Turan echoed Corliss's sentiments: "It may be unfair, but it's inevitable that *Proof of Life* is going to be seen, at least in the short run, through the lens of the offscreen romance that developed on location."

Director Taylor Hackford was particularly angered by the negative press. "I'd like *Proof of Life* to be judged on the film—not on some paparazzo view of the world!" he exclaimed.

> Of course, Russell also shared his view. But he became upset when Hackford himself blamed the movie's failure on the Crowe-Ryan affair. At a London press conference, Russell responded to Hackford's comments by saying, "The guy's an idiot. The film is what the film is. I don't think truly that the relationship had a negative effect on the movie."

Despite the critical and commercial failure of *Proof of Life*, Russell had reached a high point in his career. But winning accolades and awards as an action hero brought him only so much creative satisfaction. He still wanted to be noted as a serious actor, projecting both drama and depth in his various film portrayals.

He still wanted to be noted as a serious actor, projecting both drama and depth in his various film portrayals.

He was definitely proceeding in the right direction, but he needed one more surefire vehicle to cement his status as a Hollywood actor of substance. Who would have thought that a kid actor who had achieved prominence on such mild television fare as *The Andy Griffith Show* and *Happy Days* would provide him with the opportunity.

chapter 10

A Journey into Madness

Russell's career success coincided with the end of his personal relationship with Meg Ryan. Following production on *Proof of Life*, Russell returned to Australia to spend a traditional Christmas with his family, to which he'd invited Meg. Meg preferred to stay in the U.S. to celebrate the holidays with her son and, of course, to not take the boy away from his father, Dennis Quaid.

On Christmas Day, Russell received a telephone call from Meg informing him that she wanted to end their relationship. Russell was devastated. He immediately retreated to his room in his Australian farmhouse and did not leave for two days. Eventually, as friends arrived to share in post-Christmas celebrations, Russell recovered, though neither he nor anyone else mentioned Meg Ryan's name.

It took a while, but Russell did recover from their breakup. Almost a year later, in a December 2001 interview for *Entertainment Weekly,* he remarked about their relationship: "We fell in love. It happens—thank God. It was an incredibly intense period of my life and obviously of her life. She's a magnificent person." Russell then added, "If anything, I owe her an apology for not being as flexible as I might have been. I don't think I'll ever make that mistake again."

At this point in his life, Russell admitted that he had only fallen in love twice—with long-time sweetheart Danielle Spencer and with Meg Ryan.

> At this point in his life, Russell admitted that he had only fallen in love twice—with Danielle Spencer and Meg Ryan.

Fortunately for Russell, Danielle chose to remain in his life. Just two days after Meg's telephone call announcing their breakup, Russell called Danielle and asked her to drive the seven-hour trip from her home in Sydney to be with him. She couldn't come out immediately, but she did join up with him before the Crowe family's weeklong holiday celebration ended, and once again the two became lovers.

> Just as Russell overcame one problem, another surfaced on March 7, 2001, when it was announced that he was the target of a kidnapping threat. According to the FBI, Russell had been a target for abduction for almost a year. Most importantly, the threat had to be taken seriously in light of such high-profile celebrity stalking incidents as those surrounding Michael J. Fox and the murders of Tejano singer Selena and TV actress Rebecca Schaeffer.

Russell Crowe was thrust into the spotlight, not because of his celebrity status, but by the security that always accompanied him, most notably the attendance of the FBI at the 2001 Golden Globe Awards.

Maintaining his tough guy image, Russell publicly laughed off this threat to his well being. But it seemed agents in four different countries were aware of the kidnapping plot, and Russell felt he had to take this threat seriously.

When he arrived in Britain in March 2001 for the opening of *Proof of Life*, he was surrounded by Scotland Yard security agents. Then, two days later, Russell was back in Los Angeles, the guest of two special screenings of *Gladiator*. He also appeared at a post-Screen Actors Guild event and a next-day Oscar nominee

A Beautiful Mind (2001)

luncheon at the Beverly Hilton Hotel. At each, Russell was seen in the company of stern-looking security people.

Fortunately, the kidnapping rumors turned out to be just that. And after being the subject of protective procedures in Hollywood, London and even Sydney, Russell resumed his career.

Next on Russell's agenda was a role in his good friend Jodie Foster's proposed production of *Flora Plum,* in which he would be featured as a circus performer. Russell was enthusiastic about doing the part and threw himself into gymnastic training.

While practicing a stunt called the Spanish Web, where he climbs up two pieces of material as he would a rope, then knots the material around his ankles before falling backwards, Russell suffered an injury that landed him in the hospital. Production on the film had to be shut down, and Russell was devastated.

"There's no words to explain how embarrassed, humiliated and bereft I felt," he later said. "But I was in a massive amount of pain, and I needed and had surgery."

Flora Plum was eventually cancelled. But once he had physically recovered, Russell swiftly went back to work.

A Beautiful Mind originated as a *Vanity Fair* article that detailed a Nobel Prize-winning genius's struggle with mental illness. John Forbes Nash Jr.

was a brilliant mathematician who combated and eventually overcame intense episodes of paranoid schizophrenia.

The magazine's editor, recognizing the story's potential for a motion picture, contacted producer Brian Grazer who, with partner Ron Howard, ran Imagine Entertainment.

Ron Howard, the former Opie Taylor/Richie Cunningham, had built an impressive post-acting profession as a director. He emerged from the ranks of producer Roger Corman productions in such low-budget fare as the 1977 film *Grand Theft Auto* to carve an impressive niche for himself as the director of numerous movies, à la fellow television alumnus Rob Reiner ("Meathead" of *All in the Family*).

Perhaps Howard's best-known cinematic achievements are *Cocoon* (1985) and *Apollo 13* (1995). Howard boasted a quite impressive track record, with more successes than duds. But many in the industry still regarded him as a former "child actor" and therefore did not take him as seriously as he deserved to be. Fortunately, all that was about to change.

Brian Grazer convinced Universal Pictures to purchase the rights to make a film on Nash's life for Imagine Entertainment. Next, screenwriter Akiva Goldman, whose credits included *The Client* and *A Time to Kill* came onboard. Goldman requested the assignment because the story had personal value to him. His parents had founded a home for psychologically troubled children in Brooklyn, and he grew up surrounded by children diagnosed with schizophrenia and other mental conditions. Goldman knew he could delve into the heart of the story and draw out the truth in a realistic, non-exploitive and compassionate way.

He'd submitted the script to several potential lead actor candidates, but he kept coming back to Russell Crowe, who had intrigued him with his performance in *The Insider*.

Initially, Ron Howard remained noncommittal on

directing the movie as he was considering other assignments. However, once Grazer excitedly presented him with the script that Goldman had written, Howard jumped into the project. The screenplay represented a story with substance. It was just the type of film that appealed to Howard's creative sensibilities.

Howard knew that in order to succeed with *A Beautiful Mind*, correct casting was the most essential component. He'd submitted the script to several potential lead actor candidates, but he kept coming back to Russell Crowe, who had intrigued him with his performance in *The Insider*.

When Russell received the script, he was in Austin, Texas, recording with his band, 30 Odd Foot of Grunts. Instantly, he was intrigued both by the concept of the movie and the character he would be portraying. Russell was both fascinated and disturbed by the subject of insanity, and he quickly delved into research to such a degree that by the time he met with Ron Howard, he knew more about the John Forbes Nash character than Howard did. Howard was so impressed by this intensity of preparation that he immediately chose Russell for the role.

For other parts in the picture, Howard selected a strong supporting cast, including Christopher Plummer to play Dr. Rosen, the psychiatrist, as well as Ed Harris and Judd Hirsch. For the role of John Nash's wife Alicia, Howard decided upon Jennifer Connelly, a 31-year-old actress who, to that point, had appeared in two dozen movies, her career graduating from the forgettable

A Beautiful Mind (2001)

Creepers (1985) to perhaps her best-known role as the heroine Sarah in *Labyrinth* (1986).

During pre-production for the film, Russell offered many suggestions. One he was most adamant about was that the movie be shot in sequence, which is not the way pictures are usually shot. Chronological order of filming is generally more expensive, particularly when filming on location. Still, Russell believed that the most effective way for him to portray Nash from his younger self to his later age would be to film from the beginning of the story and proceed directly through to the end, with no breaks in continuity.

Ron Howard initially opposed the expensive proposal but then went to Universal and spoke to the bankrolling executives presenting the star's argument. Both Russell's and Ron Howard's stars had risen considerably by this time, so such decisions were acknowledged with virtually no protest from the studio.

Howard was ready to begin filming; however, he did express a tentative concern regarding Russell. "I'd talked to some of the directors who'd worked with him and heard that he can be difficult."

Russell responded directly to Howard. "I can be kind of noisy, but I don't mean to be a rude bastard. Talk to me, hear me out, because I have my ideas, too."

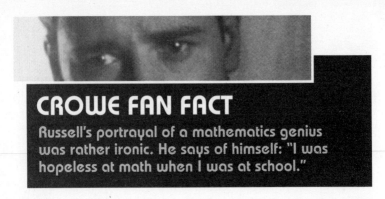

CROWE FAN FACT

Russell's portrayal of a mathematics genius was rather ironic. He says of himself: "I was hopeless at math when I was at school."

At that point, the pathways were clean, and both Russell and Howard embarked on a mutually rewarding project that solidified both of their careers.

Again, Russell embarked on extensive preparation for the role, often bordering on the eccentric, such as when he interviewed New York City street people who were not merely homeless but clearly suffering from their own emotionally instabilities. Russell absorbed many of their mannerisms and speech inflections to further his characterization of John Nash.

> Russell then drove out to Bluefield, West Virginia, to visit the town where Nash was born, to soak up atmosphere and get a feel for the environment. Unfortunately, this plan did not transpire as was hoped, because he drove into a major snowstorm that necessitated a quick return to New Jersey.

Most of the movie was filmed on location, with principal shooting taking place in New Jersey, specifically at Princeton, but with additional filming in New York City, at Manhattan College and Fordham University.

Of all his creative ventures, *A Beautiful Mind* held the most significance for Russell. Certainly from a professional standpoint, he had done no finer acting. But on a personal level, the film brought him to grips with his own childhood, where he never felt he fit into the norm. He had often wondered if he was crazy. Even his mother apparently entertained that possibility. As he grew into adulthood, he was prone to unexpected outbursts of wild behavior, often prompted by drinking bouts, that gave rise to bad press, which he regretted the next day.

> Russell understood that living the life of a celebrity was often like walking a tightrope. There is the work, which Russell maintained mattered most, but unlike a doctor, dentist, or other professional, a recognizable figure such as himself remained in the public eye—a devastating aspect of achieving creative fulfillment.

Whether or not Russell used such psychology in formulating his portrayal of John Forbes is uncertain, there is no question that what he delivered onscreen is an exceptional, compassionate performance that delved deeply and convincingly into a brilliant yet deeply disturbed mind.

Despite many of the negative aspects of that true life drama, the story ends on a positive note, all the more affecting because *A Beautiful Mind* is the representation of one man's traumatic psychological plight, from which he emerges whole because of his own resolve and with the support of his loving wife.

Of all his creative ventures, *A Beautiful Mind* held the most significance for Russell. Certainly from a professional standpoint, he had done no finer acting.

A Beautiful Mind (2001)

Madness? Perhaps the creative experience of making the picture helped to keep the potential at bay for Russell himself. On the personal front, despite Russell's romantic expectations, Danielle Spencer was excelling at her own singing and acting career and celebrated the release of her first album, *White Monkey,* which she had worked on for about three years. As she reported to the *Sydney Morning Herald,* she wanted to see her career alternate between acting and music.

Upon completion of *A Beautiful Mind* in the summer of 2001, Russell focused his attention on his own music career, this time putting together an American tour for his band. Danielle accompanied the group, undoubtedly as a way to promote *White Monkey.*

The relationship between the two looked solid—until Russell detoured into the Fiji Islands while en route to Australia for a brief visit with his family. It just so happened that Russell's friend Nicole Kidman, recently divorced from Tom Cruise, was vacationing in Fiji at the time with her two children. Apparently, pregnant Kidman was distraught over her marital breakup with Cruise, and Russell consoled her.

He and Kidman were seen socially, but they publicly denied that they were anything other than friends. This statement could have been true, since it appeared that most of Russell's attention at this time was on the launch of his band's North American tour in conjunction with the release of the album *Bastard Life or Clarity.*

There is no way to identify the musical stylings presented on the recording—perhaps, hence, the album's title. The songs are basically a compilation of Scottish and Irish folk tunes that are less rock and roll than Gaelic. Unfortunately, the album's eclectic format presented problems for public judgment when the album was released.

Scotty Moore, who had achieved prominence as one of the founders of what became known as "rock 'n roll," was initially baffled by the content, saying that he personally could not discern who the listening audience would be. The concerts that 30 Odd Foot of Grunts performed were likewise received with mixed reviews, despite the lead presence of Russell Crowe. Russell's "crusty baritone" was applauded by some, such as Ann Powers, writing for the *New York Times*, and derided by others.

> Danielle Spencer's contribution to the tour was virtually ignored. One of their few reviews simply said that she bore "a striking resemblance to Kirsten Dunst."

The North American tour did re-establish the romance between Russell and Danielle, and at the tour's end, the couple returned to Sydney where they decided to move in together, purchasing a multimillion-dollar mansion for that purpose.

It was an arrangement that was approved by both sets of parents, although Don Spencer remarked, "Russell may not be everyone's cup of tea, but he's always been fabulous to Danielle."

Meanwhile, Russell was receiving glowing reviews for his work in *A Beautiful Mind*. Stephen Hunter in his review for the *Washington Post* pulled no punches: "Russell

> Stephen Hunter in his review for the *Washington Post* pulled no punches: "Russell Crowe is fabulous."

Crowe is fabulous." Likewise, *Denver Post* reviewer Steven Rosen stated that Russell gave an "outstanding performance."

> An interesting aspect to the story, hinted upon in the film, is that John Nash may have possessed homosexual tendencies. Apparently, such accusations, perhaps arising from his schizophrenia, had been directed at him. Regardless of what may have occurred during Nash's periods of dementia, upon his eventual treatment for the disease, Nash entered into a wholly heterosexual relationship with his wife, uninterrupted by any dementia.

Russell received many accolades for *A Beautiful Mind*, though inevitably, he received his share of personal snares, including questions and comments focusing on his sexuality, as well as inquiries into his mental stability. To many it seemed as though there was no way that Russell could so effectively play a character such as John Nash unless he too possessed similar psychological quirks. The role was seen as a triumph of his acting ability, but many also thought of Russell's often-public displays of temper.

Russell generally laughed away such stories. He remained gracious with his fans, but he had little patience with the press,

> The role was seen as a triumph of his acting ability, but many also thought of Russell's often-public displays of temper.

particularly the tabloids, to whom he had become a most attractive target.

During one press conference, he was asked outright whether he felt he was edging into insanity. Russell managed to remain calm, though he bit his lip and said to the interviewer, "I know where you're going with this. Next."

Less bluntly, but more frankly, he responded to a question regarding if he thought he was misunderstood. "No, I don't think I'm misunderstood. But I think I'm misconstrued. I think it's very easy to offend people with the truth."

> He often found that he had to respond to journalists' questions with spicy answers. Of course, such replies did not endear Russell to the press. Tabloids spoke of an actor imbued with an inner rage.

"What price stardom" was a motto he refused to live by. He'd reached the heights, but there remained a few heights still left for him to mount.

in Command

The year 2002 appeared to be another bountiful year for Russell. He was a Golden Globe nominee—Best Actor for *A Beautiful Mind*. Interestingly, former flame Nicole Kidman was similarly up for two awards—Best Actress in a comedy/musical (*Moulin Rouge)* and in a drama *(The Others)*.

However, what seemed true on the surface was not necessarily the case.

Russell made the rounds of interviews to promote *A Beautiful Mind*, which was up for a Best Picture Award. Most journalists were critical of Russell, with Desmond Sampson of *Pavement* magazine writing that interviewing Russell Crowe was like going on an "emotional roller-coaster ride."

The *New Zealander* was even more precise: "Ultimately, it feels like we've just endured three rounds in the ring with Crowe, rather than enjoyed half an hour chatting with him in a swanky hotel room."

Russell had become weary and punchy. Perhaps the actor who so completely absorbed the personal traits of his myriad characters had, to a degree, become John Nash. Russell had committed himself so totally into promoting the movie that he was clearly exhausted.

His agenda also included a more modest promotion of his movie *Texas,* which was a documentary showcase of his band 30 Odd Foot of Grunts, highlighting rehearsals and international recording sessions from 2000 through 2001, reaching from Sydney and London to Austin, Texas.

Russell rightly received a co-producer credit on the film, which premiered at a midnight showing at the Sundance Film Festival in Park City, Utah, on

January 21. Russell personally attended the initial showing of *Texas*, attired in basic, common clothing—a red flannel shirt and blue jeans. He sat in the fourth row of the theater among the small audience.

Kate X. Messer writing for the *Austin Chronicle* said: "TOFOG's cinematic debut is 'two hours of mild cinematic torture.'" Perhaps Russell was upset by such negative publicity against his band.

> **If there was a guidepost in his personal life, it was his relationship with Danielle Spencer. And it was Danielle who accompanied him to the Golden Globe Awards ceremonies, where Russell was awarded the Best Actor prize for his role in *A Beautiful Mind*. Indeed, it was a beautiful moment both personally and professionally.**

Russell was also nominated for Best Actor at the British Academy of Film and Television Arts (BAFTA) Awards. A warm scenario was nearly ruined by Nicole Kidman, who made herself more than comfortable by placing her shapely body upon Russell's lap while Danielle was indisposed in the women's restroom. An uncomfortable situation indeed, but the evening concluded with Russell Crowe winning the BAFTA Best Actor award for *A Beautiful Mind*.

Russell had committed himself so totally into promoting the movie that he was clearly exhausted.

Despite this victory, Russell apparently was unhappy that a poem he had recited during his acceptance speech had been edited from the televised broadcast. Professionally affronted, Russell confronted the show's producer Malcolm Gerrie, to whom he reportedly spewed out a stream of obscenities before kicking over chairs and storming out of the room.

Such a display of temperament hardly made Russell a darling of the British press. The result was comments and insinuations regarding his impetuous, perhaps even dangerous behavior.

Russell rallied to his own defense. He reported that he had been stressed over a great many issues, including the expensive press tour he had undertaken on behalf of *A Beautiful Mind,* and was exhausted at the incessant questions regarding his own mental health. He eventually apologized to Gerrie for his attitude and even offered to buy him a few pints of Guinness the next time he was in London.

It certainly had been a busy time for Russell. Work, interviews and personal considerations kept him at a fever pitch. Still, Russell thrived on his work.

Russell became as amenable as he could be to the press. He was a major contender in the Academy Award race, as was the picture itself and its director, Ron Howard. *A Beautiful Mind* looked like a shoo-in in all the major categories. Russell appeared to be lined up to win the Academy's Best Actor award, having beat out Will Smith, Billy Bob Thornton and Kevin Spacey at the Golden Globes.

Come Oscar night, many of the results were as predicted. Ron Howard received a long-overdue Best Director Award, a bittersweet moment as his mother had recently passed away, and he accepted the acknowledgment partly in tribute to her. Akiva Goldsman also picked up a trophy for Best Screenplay Adaptation, as did Jennifer Connelly for Best Supporting Actress. Finally, *A Beautiful Mind* capped the evening by capturing the Oscar for Best Picture.

> Russell appeared to be lined up to win the Academy's Best Actor award, having beat out Will Smith, Billy Bob Thornton and Kevin Spacey at the Golden Globes.

Surprisingly, it was Russell Crowe who left the awards ceremony empty-handed, having lost the Best Actor award to Denzel Washington—a long shot, but nevertheless acknowledged by Academy voting members for his work in *Training Day*.

March 24, 2002, proved quite a night for African-Americans. Besides Denzel Washington achieving the Best Actor nod, Halle Berry received the Best Actress Oscar for *Monster's Ball*. Apparently, Academy politics had produced some prejudice in the night's awards. John Nash had supposedly made anti-Semitic comments regarding Ron Howard, which were further fueled by a ridiculous edict stating that Russell Crowe should not be allowed to win an Oscar two years in a row.

However, the truth may have been acknowledged through the purported comment of one Academy member who reported to *Entertainment Weekly* that Russell Crowe was "an obnoxious human being and an arrogant prick."

Despite the negative press, Russell still remained a strong box office commodity. He was next cast in his most adventurous role yet—the heroic Captain Jack Aubrey in *Master and Commander: The Far Side of the World*. The film was an adaptation of Patrick O'Brian's 20-volume set of seafaring stories set against the backdrop of the Napoleonic Wars.

Russell had no knowledge of these books and wasn't terribly impressed with the script that was presented to him. However, he was intrigued at the prospect of working with director Peter Weir, a fellow Australian who had amassed an impressive series of credentials, including *Dead Poets Society* (1989) and *The Truman Show* (1998).

"Peter was very inspirational to me as a young man," he said. "He is a legend around the world and actors want to work with him. I'm not an exception."

Master and Commander: The Far Side of the World (2003)

Shooting for the picture began in Mexico on June 17, 2002. Russell again endured bad publicity when he got into an altercation with a man, kissed another man and got into a fight with a woman. Apparently, all was captured on video, and a blackmail scheme was perpetrated whereby the incriminating video would be sold to Russell for a price exceeding $100,000.

Fortunately, the men were arrested and charged with extortion. Russell was out of the country and so could not be called to testify on his own behalf—which may have produced self-damning evidence.

More troubles developed when Russell was filming on location in Rosarito, Mexico, and Danielle flew in by helicopter to see him. When asked by a television interviewer whether he had truly stated that Danielle Spencer was the most beautiful woman in the universe, Russell replied: "Did I say that? If she's watching, yes, of course I did."

Danielle responded likewise, teasingly, when she appeared on the same program and was asked if she considered Russell the most beautiful man. She said, "If he's watching, absolutely."

Yet there appeared to be trouble in Paradise. Allegedly, Meg Ryan had once again entered the picture with her passion for Russell restored, sending e-mails numbering in the hundreds, pleading with him to get in contact with her.

Next, Nicole Kidman apparently appeared on the scene,

complicating the situation. Thirty-eight-year-old Russell tried to remain a gentleman while juggling three romantic scenarios.

Russell's inherent vanity helped ease the tension. He was disturbed to discover that his hair was turning gray. During the filming of *Master and Commander,* he apparently was not pleased with his make-up artist's handling of his hair. He had the employee fired and requested that the studio, Twentieth Century-Fox, fly his own personal hairdresser in from Sydney at a reported cost of more than $100,000—a princely sum, but one that the company was not reluctant to pay given Russell's screen prominence.

Master and Commander was a long, demanding shoot, taking nearly seven months to film. The movie tells the story of Captain Jack Aubrey, who sets sail to the far side of the world on the HMS *Surprise* with a crew basically made up of misfits. After many adventures at sea, including dissension among the men onboard and health hazards such as scurvy, they do battle with a French warship, the *Achelon*. While the film is not short on action, director Weir keeps the audience interested in the human interaction.

Ever the history buff, Russell threw himself into research to prepare for the role, reading about ships and battles of the period, studying seamanship and sword fighting, and learning to speak

Master and Commander: The Far Side of the World (2003)

CROWE FAN FACT

Russell secretly recorded a duet with Chrissie Hynde of The Pretenders called *Never Be Alone Again*, which is featured on TOFOG's 2003 album, *Other Ways of Speaking*.

like a Dorset-raised 18th-century British sea officer. The most challenging aspect of preparing for the film, however, was mastering the violin.

"You can take all the helicopter stunts and tiger fights and gun battles I've done for the movies, and nothing was as difficult as learning to play the violin," Russell said. "I play guitar average and drums loudly. But the violin is the harshest mistress I've met."

Russell's approach to his role and his leadership on the set earned him the respect of the cast and crew. Gordon Laco, the Toronto-based nautical expert who was the historical consultant for the film, said of Crowe, "Russell was so committed to understanding everything about Jack Aubrey that it rubbed off on everybody else on the set...It was a level of commitment I've never seen in a film project. The actors behaved like a real crew. And Russell was largely responsible."

Released in November 2003, *Master and Commander: The Far Side of the World* was Russell's third successive box office hit, drawing in a take of $210 million, a figure just slightly lower than the earnings of *A Beautiful Mind*. The picture also scored high in technical achievement, winning Oscars for cinematography and sound editing.

Following the completion of the film, an exhausted Russell took a break from moviemaking to put the finishing touches on his band's new album and to work out a concert tour schedule. Despite this brief respite from making movies, he still had a full workload ahead of him—along with a somewhat uncertain personal life. While Meg Ryan had disappeared from the picture, he was still balancing relationships with Danielle and Nicole Kidman.

The pressure once again got to him, and he became involved in another well-publicized row in London.

Russell's *Gladiator* co-star Richard Harris had recently died, and just several days after attending the wake, shortly before flying back to the United States, Russell and his bodyguards went out to dinner at a Japanese restaurant. He became attracted to a 21-year-old girl, who happened to be the daughter of British record producer Tony Calder. Russell went to her table where he attempted to get "too friendly," both kissing and licking the girl's face. When she firmly rejected his offer to go with him to his hotel room, Russell returned to his own table, where he proceeded to get into an argument with Eric Watson, who owned a championship rugby team, the Warriors. At one point, Watson went into the washroom and was followed by Russell, obviously looking for a fight. However, it was Russell who got the worst of the deal, as Watson was a skilled boxer. Someone called the police. Russell was out of control, throwing plates across the room for his bodyguard to catch. Fortunately, by the time the police arrived, the commotion had quieted, and no charges were laid, although Russell was photographed leaving the restaurant looking the worst for wear from his altercation with Watson.

While he avoided arrest, Russell had been once again caught in the center of bad publicity. He decided to cancel his commitments, including the American tour with 30 Odd Foot of Grunts, and return to Australia. He also wanted to be with Danielle.

"You can take all the helicopter stunts and tiger fights and gun battles I've done for the movies, and nothing was as difficult as learning to play the violin," Russell said.

First, however, Russell endured more negative headlines while in New York, when he reportedly lost his temper over a fruit basket that had been sent to his room. Apparently the fruit had not been cut to his precise specifications.

A newspaper report at the time also suggested that he was quitting show business to live with his parents and his "long-suffering girlfriend."

Through all the difficulty, Danielle vowed to stick by Russell. Finally, after a romantic proposal at a Sydney restaurant, Danielle agreed to marry him. The wedding date was set for April 7, 2003, Russell's 39th birthday.

The wedding was a lavish, three-day celebration for family and friends flown in from all over the world. Guests of honor included musician Sting, actress Jodie Foster, designer Giorgio Armani and Texas governor Rick Perry. For the ceremony, Russell had a chapel specially designed and built on his 800-acre ranch at Nana Glen near Coffs Harbour in northern New South Wales. His plans almost went awry when the $400,000 structure nearly had to be torn down just days before the nuptials because the impetuous actor had neglected to get a building permit. The chapel was given a reprieve after local inspectors deemed it safe and granted a last-minute permit. In preparation for the wedding, Russell filled the chapel with religious symbols from all over the world. To keep media hordes from intruding on the occasion, Russell tried to have the area over the ranch declared a "no-fly zone." However, not even his celebrity clout was enough for local officials to comply with the actor's wishes, and his request was denied.

Danielle Spencer and Russell Crowe became husband and wife in a romantic sunset ceremony that began in true Hollywood style with the groomsmen arriving on motorcycles—personal gifts from Russell. The bride and groom were both attired in Armani, Russell in a morning suit and a waistcoat embroidered with the coats of arms of both families, and Danielle in a spectacular

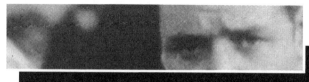

CROWE FAN FACT

At the wedding reception, Russell, accompanied by his band, 30 Odd Foot of Grunts, serenaded the bride with love songs.

gown, hand-beaded with 10,000 Swarovski crystals. The traditional ceremony also included a fertility blessing by a local Aboriginal shaman.

In contrast to the extravagant nuptials, the couple enjoyed an extended driving honeymoon through Australia. They spent a modest weekend in a motel in the Queensland town of Rockhampton, as well as Cairns and Innisfail. Two months after the wedding, the couple was expecting their first child.

"Marrying Danielle, having a home together and starting a family have been in my mind for a number of years," he said. "And the reality is far better than the idea."

A few weeks earlier than anticipated, on the evening of December 21, 2003, Charles Spencer Crowe was born in Sydney's Royal North Shore Private Hospital. After the birth, Russell "hogged" the baby, refusing to allow anyone else to hold him, telling everyone, "I'm bonding, I'm bonding." A doting and protective parent, the actor seemed determined to keep his family from the prying eyes of the media.

In 2003, Russell also began frequenting the talk show circuit, which he'd rarely done in the past, appearing on *The Oprah Winfrey Show*, *Late Night with Conan O'Brien* and *Live with Regis and Kelly*, and on January 4, 2004, he was finally awarded the privilege to expound on his theories of acting with John Lipton and acting hopefuls on Bravo's *Inside the Actor's Studio*.

taming the wild man

Russell has not retired from his film career, but he has apparently retired from his wild ways. He publicly announced that he has quit drinking, motivated by his desire to get in shape for the film *Cinderella Man*, his second film directed by Ron Howard. The movie, which started filming in late April 2004, is based on the life of Depression-era boxer James Braddock and also stars Renée Zellweger and Craig Bierko. Russell is also the executive producer for this film.

James Braddock earned himself the moniker "Cinderella Man" for his fairytale-like ascent from unknown amateur boxer to professional heavyweight boxing champion during the tough Depression years. Born to Irish immigrants in 1906 in New York City, James dropped out of school and worked odd jobs. Always a scrapper, he fought his first official amateur boxing match in November 1923. His powerful right hand helped him achieve a successful amateur career, and he turned pro in 1926. But times were hard, and Braddock struggled to earn enough from his fights to support his young family. In an historic upset in 1935, he defeated Max Baer to earn the title of Heavyweight Champion of the World—a real-life "Rocky." The working-class people of the time embraced him as a hero, an ordinary man who managed to become a champion despite the hardships of the Depression.

To prepare for his role, Russell trained with some of the foremost boxing instructors in the world, including former World

> To prepare for his role, Russell trained with some of the foremost boxing instructors in the world...

Champion Heavyweight contender Joe Bugner. Brian Grazer, one of the film's producers, stated, "I've never known any actor who dedicates himself to a part with more intensity than Russell. He approaches every role with a rigorous discipline, using his mind, his body and his spirit."

This dedication to his craft, coupled with his intense training, was likely the cause of an injury that set the filming schedule back five weeks. Russell dislocated his shoulder and required arthroscopic surgery to repair the damage. Typically, the actor approached his rehab with the same intensity that he devotes to his work and was back on the set in record time.

Because it was filmed in Toronto, Canada, *Cinderella Man* attracted the wrath of the Film and Television Acting Committee as well as the Congressional Entertainment Caucus, headed by Congresswoman Diane Watson. She fought to have the movie made at Universal Studios and accused the film studio of "placing profits over American jobs." Representatives of the studio explained that the reasons for the Canadian shoot were logistical rather than economic. Director Ron Howard defended the location decision stating that it was easier to make Toronto look like New York in the 1930s because of the availability of locations such as Maple Leaf Gardens, standing in for Madison Square Gardens, where about one-third of the movie was to be shot.

An unfortunate incident that occurred during the filming of *Cinderella Man* brought to light a side of Russell's personality not often seen. On April 5, 2004, vandals fire-bombed a Jewish school in Montreal and scrawled racist slogans on its walls. Russell, on hearing of the hate crime, offered an undisclosed amount of money to help rebuild the school's library and, with atypical modesty, asked the

"I've never known any actor who dedicates himself to a part with more intensity than Russell. He approaches every role with a rigorous discipline, using his mind, his body and his spirit."

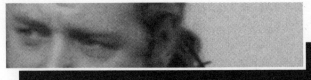

school to relay his words of support only to the students, not the general public.

Not having done a movie in Australia since *Heaven's Burning* in 1997, Russell's next project, the much-anticipated *Eucalyptus*, sees the actor return to his adopted homeland. Based on the award-winning novel by Murray Bail, the story is a quintessentially Australian one. The fable tells the tale of a widowed plantation owner, Holland, who cultivates eucalyptus trees on his property. There are hundreds of eucalyptus species, some very rare, and Holland grows every variety. When his daughter Ellen comes of age, her father decrees that she can only marry a man who can name every eucalyptus species on the plantation. Many suitors try and fail, until the arrival of Nick Cave, a botanical expert who methodically names each species. As the dry, academic Cave works his way relentlessly through the trees on the property, Ellen meets a wandering stranger, the Storyteller, who regales her, Scheherazade-like, with

> Not having done a movie in Australia since *Heaven's Burning* in 1997, Russell's next project, the much-anticipated *Eucalyptus*, sees the actor return to his adopted homeland.

tales of love and loss, each story with the theme of missed opportunities for love.

The film, scheduled to be released in 2006, will reunite Russell with director Jocelyn Moorhouse and producer Linda House, both of whom worked with Crowe on one of his earliest films, *Proof* (1991). Russell, in the role of the Storyteller, will be joined by fellow Aussies Nicole Kidman as Ellen, and Hugo Weaving, who also played in *Proof*, in the role of Nick Cave. The role of Holland was originally offered to Oscar-winner Geoffrey Rush, who starred in *Pirates of the Caribbean: The Curse of the Black Pearl* (2003) and *Quills* (2000), but he turned it down because of scheduling conflicts. Instead, Australian actor Jack Thompson will play the role. The actors are reportedly not being paid their usual Hollywood rates, but will work for Australian equity scale, a considerable cut in their usual salaries.

Despite the reams of bad press that Russell Crowe seems to generate for his allegedly wild behavior, there are also smaller stories of his kindness and philanthropy. In November 2004, he was given credit for helping save the life of a young Australian boy bitten by a venomous brown snake. The actor heard about the boy's fight for life on a newscast and contacted the child's parents to offer words of support. The parents believe that the knowledge that "the Gladiator man" was praying for their son gave the little boy extra strength and the will to live that ultimately allowed him to recover. The boy's father, Geoff Cox, stated, "If it wasn't for Russell Crowe, our little boy would be dead."

His **good deeds**, including his response to the **firebombing** of the school in Montreal rarely get the **same glaring headlines** as do his **misdeeds**.

The actor has other film projects on his agenda, including **The Long Green Shore**, based on the novel by John Hepworth, for which Russell plans to write the screenplay as well as direct. There has even been talk of sequels to **Gladiator** and **Master and Commander**. Of course he also plans to do more work with his band, recording songs and perhaps even doing some traveling. But the former wild man makes it clear that his first priority is being a husband and father.

In the motion picture industry, failure is commonplace, and Russell Crowe has defied the odds by persistently refusing to succumb to the politics of Hollywood. Driven and ambitious, he has always wanted to be successful, but has little desire for the trappings of celebrity, preferring to spend time with family on his ranch in Australia. When asked if he would ever move closer to Hollywood, he famously replied, "I'd move to Los Angeles if Australia and New Zealand were swallowed up by a huge tidal wave, if there was a bubonic plague in England, and if the continent of Africa disappeared from some huge Martian attack."

Russell is a fiercely driven perfectionist who does not suffer fools gladly. While his "bad boy" reputation is to some degree justified—the rough-and-tumble Crowe tends to react first and ponder the consequences of his actions later—he steadfastly claims that many of his indiscretions are minor incidents blown out of proportion by scandal-mongering tabloid journalists. Whatever the press may say about him, his acting talent is undeniable and he has won major awards in Australia, the U.S. and the UK. Actor, musician, cattle rancher, history buff, husband and father, Russell's frank personality forces the world to take him on his own terms, and he has emerged as a success and definitely one of the most important screen players of our generation.

RUSSELL CROWE FILMOGRAPHY

Eucalyptus (2006)

Cinderella Man (2005)

Master and Commander: The Far Side of the World (2003)

A Beautiful Mind (2001)

Proof of Life (2000)

Gladiator (2000)

The Insider (1999)

Mystery, Alaska (1999)

Breaking Up (1997)

Heaven's Burning (1997)

L.A. Confidential (1997)

Rough Magic (1995)

Virtuosity (1995)

No Way Back (1995)

The Quick and the Dead (1995)

The Sum of Us (1994)

For the Moment (1993)

The Silver Brumby (1993)

Love in Limbo/Just One Night (1993)

Romper Stomper (1992)

Spotswood (1992)

Hammers Over the Anvil (1991)

Brides of Christ—miniseries (1991)

Proof (1991)

The Crossing (1990)

Prisoners of the Sun/Blood Oath (1990)

Notes on Sources

Books

Dickerson, James L. *Russell Crowe: The Unauthorized Biography*. New York: Schirmer Trade Books, 2002.

Ewbanks, Tim and Stafford Hildred. *Russell Crowe: The Biography*. London: Carlton Books, 2001.

Wylie, Gabor H.A. *Russell Crowe: A Life in Stories*. Toronto: ECW Press, 2001.

Web Resources

Contact Music. "Russell Crowe: Artist Homepage" http://www.contactmusic.com/new/artist.nsf/artistnames/russell%20crowe.

The Internet Movie Database: Russell Crowe http://www.imdb.com.

James J. Braddock: The Official Website. http://www.jamesjbraddock.com.

Lowe, Andy. "The Rise and Rise of Russell Crowe" http://www.russellcroweheaven.com/inprint/Totalfilmjan2001

McNairy, Dave. "Pol Seeks to Keep 'Man" in States" http://www.geocities.com/Hollywood/Cinema/1501//cinderella-man/cm_inprint2

"Russell Crowe: News, Gossip and Rumors" http://www.geocities.com/Hollywood/Cinema/1501/indexnews

Snyder, Gabriel. "Injury Delays U's 'Cinderella' "
http://www.geocities.com/Hollywood/Cinema/1501//
cinderellaman/cm_inprint2

The Unofficial Russell Crowe Resource Page. "The Wit and
Wisdom of Russell Crowe"
http://www.fiktiv.com/crowe/articles/manoftheyearquotes

ICON
PRESS

STAR BIOGRAPHIES

Real stars. Real people. The life stories of show business celebrities.

LEONARDO DICAPRIO: AN INTIMATE PORTRAIT

by Colin MacLean

This book takes you beyond the screen image of Leonardo DiCaprio to provide a probing look at the serious actor who became the world's most famous movie star. Entertainment journalist Colin MacLean uses personal interviews with DiCaprio, exhaustive research and an intimate knowledge of how the Hollywood system works to chronicle the life of the outgoing kid who grew up poor in East Hollywood and who now commands $20 million a picture.

$7.95 USD/$9.95 CDN • ISBN 1-894864-21-2 • 5.25" x 8.25" • 144 pages

JOHNNY DEPP: THE PASSIONATE REBEL

by Stone Wallace

Uncovers the real man behind the media hype. Is Depp really the "bad boy" he's made out to be by the paparazzi or simply a sensitive man who likes to keep his private life private. Colleagues describe Depp as a contemporary James Dean. He's certainly one of the most eclectic and eccentric actors ever to reach the heights of super stardom. A sexy, quirky actor, Depp chooses his roles on his own terms.

$7.95 USD/$9.95 CDN • ISBN 1-894864-17-4 • 5.25" x 8.25" • 144 pages

JULIA ROBERTS: MORE THAN A PRETTY WOMAN

by Colin MacLean

Hollywood's highest-paid actress is also a fascinating, complex woman who is already a legend. Entertainment journalist Colin MacLean uses personal interviews and in-depth research to find the enigmatic, intensely insecure but dedicated artist behind the famous megawatt smile.

$7.95 USD/$9.95 CDN • ISBN 1-894864-23-9 • 5.25" x 8.25" • 144 pages

GWYNETH PALTROW: GRACE AND THE GIRL NEXT DOOR

by Glenn Tkach

The daughter of producer Bruce Paltrow and actress Blythe Danner, Gwyneth Paltrow first stepped into the media's white-hot glare during her high-profile relationship with Brad Pitt. Now an Oscar winner, a mother, a fashion cover girl and an acclaimed stage actress, Gwyneth Paltrow has managed to fly under the radar of the media and remain an enigmatic and intriguing personality.

$7.95 USD/$9.95 CDN • ISBN 1-894864-24-7 • 5.25" x 8.25" • 144 pages

ORLANDO BLOOM: SHOOTING TO STARDOM

by Peter Boer

Hard to believe now perhaps, but when British actor Orlando Bloom appeared on the silver screen as Legolas in the first of the three *Lord of the Rings* films, he was a virtual unknown in the movie industry. In this readable biography, author Peter Boer details Bloom's rise to success, starting with his humble beginnings as a clay trapper at a Canterbury gun club. The book chronicles Bloom's progress through acting schools in London and the back-breaking accident that changed the course of his life and propelled him on the path to stardom.

$7.95 USD/$9.95 CDN • ISBN 1-894864-18-2 • 5.25" x 8.25" • 144 pages

Look for books in the *Star Biographies* series at your local bookseller and newsstand or contact the distributor, Lone Pine Publishing, directly. In the U.S. call 1-800-518-3541. In Canada, call 1-800-661-9017.